WOMEN
PRIESTS:

YES
OR
NO
?

WOMEN PRIESTS:

YES
OR
NO
?

Emily C. Hewitt
Suzanne R. Hiatt

THE SEABURY PRESS
NEW YORK

ACKNOWLEDGMENT

THE AUTHORS gratefully acknowledge the contributions of time, thought, and elbow grease which others have made to this book. We thank especially Susan Eenigenburg, James B. Harrison, Carter Heyward, Susan McShane, Edna M. Pittenger, Arthur R. Buckley, and the staff of The Seabury Press.

Scriptural quotations are from the *Revised Standard Version of the Bible*, copyrighted 1946 and 1952 by the Division of Christian Education, National Council of Churches.

An Original Seabury Paperback
Copyright © 1973 by Emily C. Hewitt and Suzanne R. Hiatt
Library of Congress Catalog Number: 72–81027
ISBN: 0–8164–2076–9
Designed by NANCY DALE MULDOON
769–1272–C–5
Printed in the United States of America

CONTENTS

Contents

CHAPTER
1

LOOKING
BACKWARD

It has been a little more than fifty years since the Anglican Communion first set about to study the "proper place" of women in its life and ministry. That study itself did not spring full-blown from the head of the Archbishop of Canterbury, but had its own history of fifty prior years of debate and controversy over the proper role for deaconesses and nuns in Anglicanism. So it is safe to say that the question of the ordination of women is not a new aberration thrust upon us by the renascence of ideas of women's liberation in the 1970s.

SOLEMN ASSEMBLIES

To say we have been studying this and related questions for fifty years and more is not to say that we have reached any agreed-upon conclusions. Anglican theological inquiry on this subject has been exhaustive. In fact, a World Council of Churches gathering in 1948 remarked on the volumes of work done on the subject by Anglicans as well as on the dearth of action to implement that work.[1] A quick check of almost any of our seminary libraries will reveal shelves of books and pamphlets on the ordination of women, most showing little evidence of use. (In researching this book,

9

we came across one key document which had last been checked out to one of us ten years ago. Though the document dates from the 1930s, these were the only two dates it had ever been circulated.)

When one takes a chronological look at Anglican documents,* two interesting patterns emerge. The first is that interest in this question seems to wax and wane within the church in a way that can be directly correlated with the interest of secular society in the changing roles of women. In the church, as in secular society, interest in expanding woman's role seems strongest during and just following the great wars of the nineteenth and twentieth centuries. Perhaps women gain confidence in their ability to participate more fully in society because of the massive societal breakdown in periods of war. Wars in this century have tended to open up new vistas for women. Suddenly in an emergency society discovers that women can do all kinds of things of which they had been thought incapable, simply because those things must be done and the men are not available to do them. Both the early 1920s and the late 1940s were marked by advancements in women's political and economic rights, though in both eras women were soon sent back home by waves of returning veterans in need of their jobs.

It is clear in looking at the chronology of church studies on women that the issue of women in the church is most marked in the 1920s and the late 1940s as well as at the present time. Less was produced in the 1930s and the 1950s, and by and large documents from those eras seem to retreat from earlier affirmations of the role of women.

It was in the 1940s in a wartime emergency situation that the first woman priest was ordained in the Anglican Communion in the Hong Kong Diocese of the Holy Catholic Church in China. She was forced to resign her orders, not

* See Appendix A.

by the people among whom she had served, but by outraged English bishops. Anglicans did not deal seriously with the question again until the 1960s, when that same see, the Synod of Hong Kong and Macao, this time under the leadership of another bishop, persistently began raising the question again. Now, nearly twenty-five years later, there are again women priests in the Diocese of Hong Kong.

The second pattern that emerges when one looks at the chronology of Anglican debate on this subject is that over the years we have engaged in a kind of Alphonse-Gaston minuet over who should have jurisdiction. Time and again studies have concluded with a call for further study. A brief review of the most recent debate in our own church will serve as a case in point.

The 1964 General Convention at St. Louis changed the canon on deaconesses to read "ordered" where it had previously read "appointed." On the basis of that change, Bishop James Pike of California appointed a deaconess to be in charge of a parish, since he considered her to be ordained. He underlined this action by conferring on her in a ceremony the stole and New Testament, traditional marks of the diaconate.

The resultant furor led the House of Bishops meeting in 1965 to commission a study on the larger question of the role of women in ministry. This commission on "The Proper Place of Women in the Ministry" made a preliminary report to the House of Bishops at their 1966 meeting and recommended that study be continued. The bishops referred the matter for further study and asked that the subject be debated at the 1968 Lambeth Conference of world Anglican bishops. Lambeth did take it up, but referred it back to the national churches for further study.

The South Bend Convention of 1969 set up a Joint Commission on Ordained and Licensed Ministries to report back to the next or a subsequent convention. This commission reported to the 1970 Houston Convention, recommending the full and immediate ordination of women. A resolution embodying the recommendations of the commission report was voted down in the clergy order of the House of Deputies. The House of Bishops agreed to discuss the matter at their 1971 meeting. When the matter came up at that meeting, the bishops decided it needed further study and referred it to yet another commission. And that is where the matter stands at this writing.

MEANWHILE, BACK IN THE CHURCH

So the church has debated and referred the question for so long that it is acquiring a certain amount of expertise in putting it off. However, life goes on and the witness of women in the ministry and in the world grows ever more insistent. In 1958, in an apparently quiescent period of the debate, Episcopal Theological School in Cambridge took an important but not widely noticed step. The school changed its policy to admit women and non-postulants as degree candidates for the Bachelor of Divinity degree, the standard professional degree for ordained clergy. Though other seminaries of the Episcopal Church had from time to time admitted women as special students and had granted other degrees to women, ETS was the first to admit a number of women on the same basis as men and to do so as a matter of policy. There was no talk of ordaining women in the rationale for the move. It was justified on the simple basis that theologically educated women were needed in the Episcopal Church, especially in the then expanding fields of college work and specialized ministries.

During the 1960s as other seminaries began to admit women, signs of an actual if not a theoretical change in the ministry of women continued. The two church-sponsored training houses for women workers, Windham House in

New York and St. Margaret's House in California, closed during the decade as a result of decreased enrollments. Many of their potential students chose seminary instead. The number of women choosing the order of deaconess or applying for certification as professional church workers declined, as women working for the church began to carve out new and more independent roles for themselves. As they became as well educated as the clergy with whom they worked, it became increasingly clear that women were hindered from doing those things they'd been trained to do by their lack of the official sanction of ordination.[2]

At this writing, all Episcopal seminaries admit women students. A few do not allow them to study for the Master of Divinity degree (which has recently replaced the B.D. as the standard degree for clergy), and some have only one woman student. But the educational bars to women in the ministry have quietly been removed in the last decade, despite the prolonged and inconclusive debate on the parliamentary level. There are an increasing number of women in the church who are fully qualified educationally for ordination to the priesthood.

But the most remarkable development in the midst of all the recent debate has come as a result of the action of the Houston Convention clarifying the status of women in the diaconate. From the late nineteenth century on, the status of deaconesses had been unclear in the official mind of the church (though very clear in the minds of the deaconesses), and they were regarded as clergy in some dioceses, as lay ministers in others. Lambeth 1968 cleared the way for deaconesses to be declared within the diaconate and thus for women to be ordained deacons. The Houston Convention made the necessary canon changes to implement that understanding of women in the diaconate, with the added provision that women deacons shall meet the same requirements for ordination as men.

Prior to the Houston Convention there were about seventy deaconesses in the American church. Many of these women were retired after long and valiant service to the church, but there were few young women serving in this order of ministry. In the two years since Houston and the recognition that women deacons are in the same clergy order as men deacons, there have been nearly twenty women ordained deacons in the American church. Though exact numbers are unavailable because figures are constantly changing, there are now about fifty more women in the process of applying for Holy Orders in approximately thirty dioceses.

Thus, though the debate on the ordination of women has not moved far, the situation of women in the church has been quietly changing over the past decade. Almost unnoticed, women were canonically enabled to serve as lay readers by the 1969 Convention in South Bend. This was followed by their admission to the House of Deputies at Houston and the recognition that they may be ordained to the diaconate. With these developments, the debate over the ordination of women to the priesthood has subtly shifted from abstract questions to the reality of particular, qualified women deacons questioning the limitations on their ministries.

THE SHADOWS OF REALITIES

The debate on the place of women in the church has continued, but in the last few years events rather than pronouncements have shrunk the debate to one area alone. Though women are still badly outnumbered by men at all decision-making levels of church life, there remains no theoretical barrier to their participation except at the level of admission to the priesthood. Women may serve as delegates to diocesan and national conventions; as diocesan council, committee, and standing committee members; and in many parishes (though by no means all), as vestry members, and senior and junior wardens. We also have woman acolytes, crucifiers, lay readers, and deacons. Some of these developments are very recent and new roles for women remain unimplemented, but in many parishes and most dioceses they are theoretically possible. In the American Episcopal Church, only the priesthood—and by implication the episcopacy—remains closed to persons of the female sex regardless of qualifications or vocation.

Today the ground of the debate on the proper place of women in the ministry has shrunk to whether they should or should not be barred from the priesthood. Though an increasing number of Episcopalians are engaging in this debate, it is interesting to note that it is difficult to predict who will be for, and who will be opposed to, the ordination of women. In most matters that come before the church for debate and action, clear alliances of like-minded people can be identified. Often the Anglo-Catholics, the evangelicals, the liberals, the conservatives, the blacks, the whites, the clergy, the laity, the women, the men, the youth, the elderly can be expected to have views as a group on a particular issue. The issue of the ordination of women to the priesthood seems to cut across all these or similar groupings. While capable of raising the most heated discussions, this issue does not on the whole seem to be a vehicle for factional strife along any familiar lines. Perhaps this is because the issue is so emotionally charged and highly personalized that each person has to work out his or her own position in an individual way.

The emotional nature of the issue has been suggested by the late C. S. Lewis:

With the Church . . . we are dealing with male and female not merely as facts of nature but as the live and awful shadows of realities utterly beyond our control and largely beyond our direct knowledge. Or rather, we are not dealing with them but (as we shall soon learn if we meddle) they are dealing with us.[3]

We differ with Lewis in this: we are convinced that any "awful shadows of realities" which impinge on the debate over the ordination of women to the priesthood should be named and discussed. In fact, we believe that they should be emphasized. They should be emphasized because the "old" arguments against women in the priesthood—biblical, theological, ecumenical, practical—not only fail to convince, they often obscure good reasons for opening the priesthood to those women who are called to serve.

We therefore preface our discussion of the traditional arguments against women in the priesthood with an exploration of some emotional and psychological attitudes toward priesthood and toward women, which may be—in Lewis' words—"dealing with us" in the debate.

CHAPTER
2

WOMAN'S
PLACE

That men and women have basic physical differences is a fact which cannot be denied. It is when we begin to discuss the consequences of those differences in the way our lives are lived that we come to that troublesome area known as the "woman problem." We have somehow arrived at the notion that the best way to order society is to divide the tasks of living into two spheres, masculine and feminine. The most convenient way to do this is to circumscribe what is proper for one sex and to make everything else the realm of the other sex. In the case of our society, we have circumscribed what is proper for women and left the rest for men.

The problem we now face is that the old patterns are changing and we can no longer be as clear as we once were about which sex should do what. In fact, sex is proving diminishingly effective as a way to organize society. However, the old ideas persist and we define the resulting confusion as the "woman problem." Can women take on new roles and tasks in society and still retain their "femininity"? This question is a source of great anxiety as a quick perusal of the books and magazines beamed toward the women's market will show.

Dorothy Sayers, in an essay entitled "Human—Not Quite Human," has dramatized the plight of the woman trying to change her role in the previously all-male world of work. She suggests how it might be if men were under the same kind of pressure both to be productive and to retain their "masculinity."

Probably no man has ever troubled to imagine how strange his life would appear to himself if it were unrelentingly assessed in terms of his maleness: if everything he wore, said, or did had to be justified by reference to female approval; if he were compelled to regard himself, day in and day out, not as a member of society, but merely . . . as a virile member of society. . . . If he were vexed by continual advice how to add a rough male touch to his typing, how to be learned without losing his masculine appeal, how to combine chemical research with seduction, how to play bridge without incurring the suspicion of impotence. . . .

In any book on sociology he would find, after the main portion dealing with human needs and rights, a supplementary chapter devoted to "The Position of the Male in the Perfect State." His newspaper would assist him with a "Men's Corner," telling him how, by the expenditure of a good deal of money and a couple of hours a day, he could attract the girls and retain his wife's affection. . . . People would write books called, "History of the Male," or "Males of the Bible," or "The Psychology of the Male," and he would be regaled daily with headlines, such as "Gentleman-Doctor's Discovery," "Male-Secretary Wins Calcutta Sweep," "Men Artists at the Academy." [1]

In short, men would become embroiled in the "man problem" and the related question of the proper place for men in society.

Sayers' wit dramatizes the added burden that women face when the society changes and their time-honored sphere changes with it. We are in the midst of such change today and the question of woman's place has never been more discussed or contested. But while the debate rages about what women *should* be doing in the world, what they are *in fact* doing continues to change dramatically. Women are entering every sphere of human endeavor. They do so, however, not with the blessing of society, but with the apprehension that they are losing their unique gift of femininity. Many caution that women, though by no means inferior to men, are profoundly different from them and that their entering the world of work on an equal basis with men is courting disaster.

The insistence that women are not inferior but simply different from men in profound and irreducible ways has a disquietingly familiar ring. It reminds us of the "separate but equal" doctrine in education which this country devoutly cherished for so many years. The evidence was clear that separate never meant equal in the quality of the education of black and white children. Finally, in 1954, the Supreme Court admitted that fact, thereby reversing a whole string of its own previous decisions.

Many observers have pointed out the remarkable parallels between the arguments used to keep blacks in their place and those used to keep woman in hers. Gunnar Myrdal, in an Appendix to his landmark study of the Negro in America, has this to say:

As in the case of the Negro, women themselves have often been brought to believe in their inferiority of endowment. As the Negro was awarded his "place" in society, so there was a "woman's place." In both cases the rationalization was strongly believed that men, in confining them to this place, did not act against the true interest of the subordinate groups. The myth of the "contented women," who did not want to have suffrage or other civil rights and equal opportunities, had the same social function as the myth of the "contented Negro." In both cases there was probably—in a static sense—often some truth behind the myth.[2]

Yet, like blacks, women have been leaving "their place" in droves. In the thirty years between 1940 and 1970 the number of women working outside the home in the United States more than doubled. In 1968, 37 percent of the

American work force was female, with the large share of those workers married women. Since the percentage of women in the work force has been increasing steadily in that thirty-year period, it is very probable that at this writing it is close to 40 percent.[3]

NOBODY'S HOME AT WOMAN'S PLACE

Whatever moral judgment we would make about woman leaving the home, facts clearly demonstrate that whether she should or not, she has already left. In 1969, 30 percent of mothers of preschool children were working outside the home.[4] Many of them don't have to work for economic reasons. The vast majority of women are employed at low-skilled, low-paid jobs. In fact, during this thirty-year period of expanded employment for women, the percentage of women to men in all professional and technical positions dropped from 45 percent in 1940 to 38 percent in 1966.[5]

Caroline Bird points out that women—many of them working mothers—make an incalculable contribution to the economy. If married women who don't have to work were to drop out of the labor force, Bird suggests, bedlam would ensue in the offices and factories where women handle the paper work. Furthermore, Bird estimates that $100 billion or more, representing the money women both earn and spend, would be lost to the economy. She concludes, "Without quite realizing it, we have come to depend on a work force of married women who do not think of themselves as workers and are not treated seriously on the job." [6]

Women, like blacks, are no longer staying in their place. Yet women still have a strong emotional need to conform to feminine models. Most women feel they are working as a sacrifice for the welfare of their families rather than for career goals of their own.

As women have left the home, whatever may have been their reason for doing so, the very fact of their being in "man's world" has laid to rest many of the old arguments that they were not suited for certain kinds of work, or that they could not cope with certain kinds of environments. It is unnecessary to devote pages here to arguments about whether or not women can handle the duties of any job. As they have engaged in every imaginable kind of work, the world has discovered that the question is not what women *can* do, but what is considered *proper* for them to do.

Also, as women have left the home to work, many of them have found themselves in positions of leadership and authority in their employment. Increasingly, women are finding themselves heads of households as well. In 1968, more than 10 percent of American homes were female-headed.[7] Whatever the reasons for this—death, divorce, desertion—women are learning to cope with independence and its attendant duties and joys. While the American dream family as seen in the media still remains father, non-working mother, and two young children, the actual situation in a growing number of American homes is very different. Women today are not only gainfully employed most of their lives, but increasingly they are also the sole support for dependents and the heads of households.

THE WILL OF GOD AND WORKING WOMEN

Everything that is does not have the blessing of God, and many churchpeople react with horror to the above facts and figures. Does God want to see women, especially young mothers, working outside their homes? Does God approve of women having lives and careers of their own, independent of their husbands, fathers, and brothers? Does God approve of women having authority over other women and even men in offices, factories, hospitals, and churches?

If we answer these questions negatively, then clearly the church has been silent about a situation abhorrent to God for a very long time. Many nineteenth-century churchmen tried to stem the folly of woman's "emancipation," as the suffrage movement was called. The Rev. Jonathan F. Stearns, a Newburyport, Massachusetts, clergyman stated in an 1837 anti-suffrage pamphlet the position of those churchmen who felt that woman's place was ordained by God to be in the home:

That there are ladies who are capable of public debate, who could make their voice heard from end to end of the church and the senate house, that there are those who might bear a favorable comparison with others as eloquent orators, and who might speak to better edification than most of those on whom the office has hitherto devolved, I am not disposed to deny. The question is not in regard to *ability*, but to decency, to order, to christian propriety. . . .[8]

Stearns and his colleagues waged a long battle to keep women at home, in the fervent conviction that it was the will of God that they stay there. However, it must be conceded that in large measure they lost that battle, as the figures on women who are not at home indicate. As we shall see in the next chapter, Stearns's spiritual descendants have been forced to fight, not to keep women out of the world of work per se, but to preserve an ever shrinking male preserve. The argument about Christian propriety remains, but the battleground has shrunk to the sacred priesthood itself.

CHAPTER
3

ANYPLACE
BUT
HERE

Though the matter of "woman's place" is far from settled in the minds of many churchpeople, we live in a world where women are theoretically free to compete with men in every realm and to follow whatever calling may present itself to them. The major exception to this rule, however, is that women are not even theoretically free to exercise a sacradotal ministry in a number of the world's Christian denominations. In this chapter we will look at some of the possible reasons for this exclusion that have to do with the way we think about priesthood. In the next chapter we will look for some possible explanations that have to do with the way we think about women.

We will not consider here the biblical and theological reasons offered for excluding women from priesthood, but rather inquire into some of the assumptions churchpeople make about priests and about women which tend to color their theological inquiry without their even realizing it. In order to look objectively at the traditional arguments, we must first become aware of the part that unarticulated feelings may play when the question of women in the priesthood is considered.

We might expect that those who oppose ordination of

women to the priesthood on the grounds that women are admonished by Paul to be silent and submissive would be out crusading to get women out of the work force and back home. Doubtless, some opponents of women in priesthood accept women working outside the home as a necessary evil. But many people who oppose women in the priesthood encourage and respect women in other professions. Many acknowledge as well the tremendous contribution of lay professional church workers who are women, and revere for their skill and dedication the women deacons and nuns who serve the church.

Somehow the priesthood is "different." There are in fact among the opponents of the ordination of women priests a number of professional women. They would not think of denying qualified women access to their own professions, yet they maintain that priesthood is for men only. Many Christians feel that in this realm alone the freedom of women to pursue diverse vocations should not apply.

That priesthood is not "just another profession" is a widely held view among Christians. For this reason, many people have no difficulty drawing the line and asserting that, although they are firmly committed to women in work and professions, things are going too far when we start tampering with the sacred. Women are fine (or at least all right) everywhere else, but please, not here.

Some people accept as axiomatic the idea that priesthood is a vocation to which God simply does not call women. Thus, when women claim to have priestly vocations, many are offended and decide that the claimants are confused, blasphemously mistaken, or deliberately using the priesthood to further the aims of the women's liberation movement. Their angry response is that priesthood is sacred and therefore totally removed from whatever one might feel about woman's place in the world.

What is it about priesthood that makes it a separate case

from other professions? In this chapter we deal with three facets of people's feelings about priesthood that make them see it as "different." The first is a deep-seated reverence for male priests as "keepers of the mysteries," the second is nostalgia for the Victorian church, and the third is adherence to patriarchy as the proper way to organize society.

MAGIC AND WOMAN: A BAD COMBINATION

Magic, or mystery, is a basic component in most religious belief. This is especially so among catholic Christians, who see in the central sacrament of the Eucharist a mystical communion among the people and between the people and God. The central figure in this mystery is of course the celebrant. At the moment of consecration, the celebrant is the pivotal figure, mediating among the believers of all times and places and between the believers and God. Whatever rite: St. John Chrysostom, Prayer Book 1928, or Green Book 1970; whatever vestments: cope and mitre or sports clothes; at that moment the priest represents all of the people to each other, all of the people to God, and God to all of the people.

Exactly how this can be is one of the central mysteries of the faith, and the person of the priest is caught up in the mystery. From the days when their neighbors had their own magical rites which involved female gods and female mediators of those gods, the people of both the Old and New Israel have been wary of having women involved in their mysteries.

Certain primitive tribes fear that women are a source of "bad mana," or malevolent magic, and exclude them from religious ceremonials. The ancient Hebrews were of this persuasion, and their spiritual descendants have kept the tradition that associates women with bad magic alive into the present day. This tradition is seen in the exhaustive proscriptions of Leviticus, and is found in other parts of the Bible as well. Among the Apocryphal writings, Ecclesiasticus suggests that woman is associated with evil propensities by her very nature: "From a woman sin had its beginning and because of her we all die" (25:24). "For from garments comes the moth, and from a woman comes wickedness. Better is the wickedness of a man than a woman who does good; and it is woman who brings shame and disgrace" (42:13–14).

That women still meant bad magic in Jesus' time is seen by the proscriptions that surrounded their public life. The disciples were horrified to discover Jesus talking with a woman (John 4:27) because rabbis were forbidden to speak even with their wives in public, lest they be defiled. In a society where men were warned against teaching their daughters to read the Torah, Jesus defended the right of Mary of Bethany to learn from him. In a society where women were not accepted as legal or religious witnesses, women discovered the empty tomb.

It would appear that Jesus was trying to discourage the ancient association of women with bad magic, but that part of his ministry has yet to be fulfilled. How fully Christians have appropriated the ancient tribal prohibitions can be seen in a quotation attributed to St. John Chrysostom:

It is not good to marry. What else is woman but a foe to friendship, an inescapable punishment, a necessary evil, a natural temptation, a desirable calamity, a delectable detriment, an evil of nature, painted with fair colors.

This passage was quoted by the authors of *Malleus Maleficarum*, a fifteenth-century handbook for witch-hunters commissioned by Pope Innocent VIII and endorsed by the faculty of the University of Cologne.[1] Perhaps no more poignant and cruel illustration of the power of the association of women with bad magic exists than the history of witchcraft and the men who rooted it out, from the middle ages through the eighteenth century. Nowhere will we find more virulent fantasies about the wicked powers of women than in the proceedings of the witch trials.

Even in our own overrational age, the medium of the all-male priesthood continues to convey the ancient message that women and mystery are a dangerous combination. Though not as boldly stated as in past generations, the notion that women are bearers of bad magic and therefore dangerous persists. That bad magic is associated with woman's sexual functions can be seen in such traditions as that which forbids woman's entrance to the sanctuary in some churches because she might be menstruating and therefore "unclean."

While deploring such superstitious proscriptions, some Christians have their own way of protecting the sacrament from the possible danger of woman's evil aura—namely, restriction of the priesthood to the male sex. It is interesting to note in this regard that every other office in the Episcopal Church, including the diaconate, is technically open to women. It is also interesting to observe that churches in which the sacraments and ritual are less emphasized have been much quicker to admit women to full liturgical participation than the more catholic churches. It is only the sacred and mysterious priesthood that is considered unfit for women. We cannot help but wonder if this attitude reaches back to a long-standing fear of the potentially evil power of women.

THE CHURCH AND THE GOOD OLD DAYS

A second and more peculiarly Anglican reason why people tend to react negatively to the priesting of women is rooted in the way they view the place of religious ceremony in their lives. In addition to being a means for them to participate in mysteries that have a deep meaning historically and psychically, for most people church has a deep nostalgic significance as well. They feel part of the communion of saints at the Eucharist, but they also take comfort from their attendance at church in the thought that, here at least, all is not changed. Though the world and peoples' lives are changing at an obscenely accelerated rate, at least the church, with its familiar rituals, recalls happier days. The traditions they've known and loved from childhood are a great comfort in a world their grandparents would not recognize.

Nostalgia differs from love of tradition in that what churchpeople are nostalgic for and label "traditional" is not the church as it has been through the ages. (See Chapter 7 for a fuller discussion of tradition.) Indeed, the tradition of the church has been so widely divergent at different times and places that it is hard to imagine how twentieth-century Christians could recapture the Tradition, or even be eager to do so. How could people worship in a church in which the liturgy was in a language and form they could not comprehend?

Nostalgia is rather for the church Christians knew as children, or the church their parents and grandparents told them they knew and about which they read in nineteenth- and twentieth-century novels. Thus, though the Victorians are long gone, it is the Victorian church for which people long.

Episcopalians are especially prone to this sort of nostalgia, probably because the Victorian era was the golden age for the Episcopal Church, both in England and, more especially, in this country. Many Episcopalians still worship in (and struggle to maintain and heat) the great edifices that their Victorian grandfathers sacrificed to build. Many vestments, hymns, and prayers are Victorian in style and language (their origins are, of course, in most cases much more ancient, but the form in which we receive them is nineteenth century).

The image of the ideal priest is also affected by this nostalgia. Episcopalians hear of the great Phillips Brooks and his illustrious contemporaries and are sad that the church seems no longer to produce such giants. On the more parochial level, many people are familiar with parish legends of great priests of another day: "I still remember the days when Father So-and-so was here. Now there was a priest. He never stood for any nonsense from the children. You can be sure they were quiet when he was preaching."

The ideal Victorian priest they long for resembles Bishop Brooks in many important ways. He is a strong but gentle father figure, learned but compassionate, a gentleman in the very best sense of the word. He doesn't stand for nonsense, and indeed his presence is so commanding that the question of "nonsense" seldom, if ever, arises. He is a good preacher, a competent administrator, has a beautiful speaking voice, and is always available for pastoral or social calls.

Reason tells us, unfortunately, that such a paragon could only flourish in a calmer and more gracious age than this one. Still, in their hearts, Episcopalians keep hoping and want their church to restore as much as possible those happily remembered days. Those days were not as blissful as they recall, but memory is kind and nostalgia is the kindest of memories.

Perhaps it is nostalgia that produces a hint of annoyance in the work of so many opponents of the ordination of women to the priesthood. English scholars especially often seem irritated—even as they discuss the question—that all this modern nonsense about women should have crept into the church at all. How much more seemly it would be if churchwomen could behave like Victorian ladies. With the exception of a few malcontents like Florence Nightingale, those women never dreamed of questioning their time-honored role in church life. Had we not in the nineteenth

century rediscovered the beauties of medieval monasticism
and the ancient order of deaconesses? Either of these should
certainly be vocation enough for a woman.

At a time when the Victorian attitude toward women is
virtually dead in society, there are those in the church who
strive to preserve it. They do so not out of malice, but because they long to preserve in the church at least the gentler
virtues of another age. And so they resist changes in the
priesthood, because such changes would signal finally the
end of that age.

A MAN'S HOME IS HIS CASTLE

A third reason people see the priesthood as "different" from
other professions and therefore properly closed to women
is related to the other two. Because of the uneasy feeling
that women mean bad magic and the identification with
Victorian life, the church has come to be the prime de-
fender of the patriarchal family pattern. Though contemporary society is experimenting with a variety of domestic patterns, churchpeople seem locked in the notion that
the patriarchal pattern inherited from Ancient Israel is,
with nineteenth-century adjustments, the only way to live.

Opponents of the ordination of women often point out
that Christ is the head of the church in the same way that
father is the head of the family. Therefore, they argue, since
priests represent Christ in the church and are on earth the
heads of their congregations, a woman can no more be a
priest than a woman can head a Christian household.

That women do head Christian households is no answer
to this line of thought. Such households are seen as re-
grettable exceptions to the general rule that homes, like
churches, are rightly headed by men. The pattern of the
patriarchal nuclear family has been lifted over a period of
years to the position of a basic tenet of the Christian faith.
Though Christians in other times and places have ordered

their domestic lives in a wide variety of ways, people persist in thinking that the "ideal Christian family" must conform to a patriarchal pattern. The pattern includes a strong, firm father whose authority is unquestioned by the rest of the family. His wife is a gentle and compassionate mother who lives to serve her family and support her husband in his vocation in the world. The children in this family are happy, obedient, and well loved and understood by their parents.

The way to set a standard is to live it. Therefore the church attempts to approximate the "ideal" family both in its own internal organization and in the domestic life of its clergy. But, in this streamlined age, it isn't easily done. The bishop, rather than being the strong father in God to his people and clergy, becomes the harassed bureaucrat who is impossible to see due to his heavy schedule. The parish priest finds himself caught in the same dilemma and discovers that he cannot function as the strong wise father in his own family, not to mention his parish family. The patriarch could handle a nomadic tribe, but he has trouble keeping tabs on the comings and goings of all his dependents in a pluralistic society.

If the church should be a model of the ideal domestic arrangement for the faithful, and if that arrangement is patriarchal, then women should not be priests. Women in the priesthood would be a powerful symbolic blow to the ideal of patriarchy. They would be a direct attack on the pattern in a way that women in professions, and even in leadership roles and authority positions in the world, cannot begin to approach. If patriarchy is the Christian pattern, the priesthood must remain "different" from other areas of life by continuing as a male preserve.

Raising the question of women in the priesthood allows us to examine some assumptions about what the church, and specifically the priesthood, should be. Let us now consider some assumptions about women.

CHAPTER
4

THE
MANLY
ART
OF
SELF-DEFENSE

In the preceding chapter we have been probing some of the possible reasons why Christians might consider the priesthood "different" and therefore not open to women as other professions are. Here we will explore some unarticulated attitudes about women and their "difference" that might make them unsuitable for priesthood. The first of these is that woman's nature is basically different from man's—that she is not and cannot be a female human being, but is rather of a different order altogether from man and properly subordinate to him.

Theologically, the basis for this position is held to be in the creation narratives of Genesis 1–3. We will deal with those narratives in another chapter. At this point we will examine not the theological, but the anthropological and psychological basis for man's age-old contention that woman is more different from him than she is like him.

It is with some hesitancy that we delve into this area at all, for the dynamics of the man-woman relation are complex. The danger of oversimplification, misrepresentation, and misunderstanding of these dynamics is enormous and probably unavoidable.

Our experience as women clergy and our human intuition give us every reason to believe that man's deepest feelings about woman may well be basic to the discussion of women in the priesthood. Many objections to women priests are not rational, hence for either side to "win" the debate by means of rational argument changes few minds and fewer hearts. Perhaps Anglicans' inability to deal decisively with the question over such a protracted period of time has been rooted in our reluctance to broaden the inquiry to more basic problems of man-woman relations.

We will concentrate on male rather than female attitudes for two reasons. First, we suspect that female attitudes are apt to be derivative from male attitudes—that women tend to view life as men would like them to. Second, it is men who at present control the church's policy and practice and it is therefore men who prevent and delay fuller participation by women. Why they should feel it necessary or advisable to do so is the central question of this chapter.

WOMAN AS A NECESSARY EVIL

Anthropologists and psychiatrists have observed that men are attracted to and repelled by women at the same time. These simultaneous feelings lead to confusion and ambivalence. Sigmund Freud expressed his confusion about women when he wrote in a private letter to a woman colleague: ". . . the great question . . . which I have not been able to answer despite my thirty years of research into the feminine soul, is 'What does a woman want?' " [1]

Man's confusion about woman and how he relates to her has been the theme of much of the world's great literature. Women are adored as angels and denounced as demons,

often within the same play or poem. D. H. Lawrence describes the variety of ways in which man sees woman:

> Man is willing to accept woman as an equal, as a man in skirts,
> as an angel, a devil, a baby-face, a machine, an instrument, a
> bosom, a womb, a pair of legs, a servant, an encyclopaedia, an
> ideal or an obscenity; the one thing he won't accept her as is a
> human being, a real human being of the feminine sex.[2]

Man's ambivalence toward woman is complicated, but
running through it is a strain of antipathy. Dislike is expressed both in man's most lavish praise of woman and in
his most savage attacks on her character. The noted psychiatrist Karen Horney, in an essay devoted to this topic,
has said:

> Is it not really remarkable . . . that so little recognition and
> attention are paid to the fact of men's secret dread of women?
> It is almost more remarkable that women themselves have so
> long been able to overlook it. . . . The man on his side has in
> the first place very obvious strategic reasons for keeping his
> dread quiet. But he also tries by every means to deny it even to
> himself. . . . We may conjecture that even his glorification of
> women has its source not only in his cravings for love, but also
> in his desire to conceal his dread. A similar relief, however, is
> also sought and found in the disparagement of women that men
> often display. . . . The attitude of love and adoration signifies:
> "There is no need for me to dread a being so wonderful, so
> beautiful, nay, so saintly." That of disparagement implies: "It
> would be too ridiculous to dread a creature who, if you take her
> all round, is such a poor thing." [3]

It is remarkable that American society, which is more than
50 percent female, is so accepting of misogyny. In the church
especially we have observed that clergy who clearly do not
like women are not only fully accepted both socially and
professionally, but their blatant distaste for women is regarded as an amusing quirk of personality. "Father So-and-so
never comes to the ECW meetings. He says he has enough

trouble without having to keep the hens from pecking each other." If a person were to speak of blacks or Indians with the same disdain many men show for women, others would be seriously alarmed at his racism. But misogyny is not regarded by society as pathological.*

Once we have observed that man is ambivalent toward woman, we can begin to suggest some possible roots for his anxiety. Why do men sometimes, even often, simply not like women?

THE TWO FACES OF MOTHER

Psychiatrists tell us that our earliest experiences in life are the most important, since the way in which our emotions are dealt with at the earliest stages of development sets the tone for the rest of our lives. For this reason the first place to look in examining the way we feel about women is into our relationship as infants to our mothers. Cultures all over the world have extolled that relationship in their art forms with sensitive portrayals of mother and child. Our own Christian heritage and the veneration of Mary, the mother of God, throughout the centuries springs immediately to mind. Mother and child is such a universal expression of human love that it is no wonder so much great art centers on this theme.

For men and women alike, our first love was our infant love for our mothers. But alas for mother, our first experience of rejection, however gentle and well meant, was also at her hands, or more accurately at her breast. Erik Erikson suggests that sin first enters an infant's world when, with the advent of teething, he inadvertently bites his mother and she reacts by starting to wean him. (Apparently even for bottle-fed babies, teething and weaning come close to-

* Misandry, a dread of and aversion to men on the part of women, is less well known. It *is* considered pathological.

gether, and the baby conflates the emotional pain of weaning with the physical pain of teething.)

Erikson further suggests that "This earliest catastrophe
in the individual's relation to himself and to the world is
probably the ontogenetic contribution to the biblical saga
of paradise, where the first people on earth forfeited forever
the right to pluck without effort what had been put at their
disposal; they bit into the forbidden apple, and made God
angry." Though a mother who is aware of these dynamics
can help make the process less frustrating for a child than
it might otherwise be, nevertheless, Erikson continues,
". . . even under the most favorable circumstances, this
stage leaves a residue of a primary sense of evil and doom
and of a universal nostalgia for a lost paradise." [4]

It is no accident that Eve, "the mother of all living,"
takes the rap for the fatal bite in the Genesis story. In our
unconscious all of us blame our mothers for betraying our
love by insisting we face the larger and more hostile world.
Thus everyone—man and woman—both loves and hates
his mother. Since she was our earliest experience with
woman we tend to project our ambivalence onto all the
women we subsequently meet. In the case of women, this
ambivalence is turned inward.

Of course the dislike we feel toward mother is unconscious, and we try to compensate by honoring motherhood
and assuring girl children that the highest calling for a
woman is to be a mother. But we can't quite bring it off,
for we don't totally admire mother, but also fear and resent
her. Thus while we pay lip service to our admiration of the
state of motherhood, mother is the most maligned person
in our society.

One of the most biting attacks on mother ever written is
Philip Wylie's *Generation of Vipers*. It is a denunciation
of the American "Mom," blaming all the country's ills on
her and the way she raises her sons. Wylie's vicious rantings

about Mom strike a responsive chord in the American heart because he says things we'd all vaguely felt but had never dared say.

Society's hostility to mother is also seen in the impossible role she is expected to fill. Psychiatrists and educators tell her repeatedly how important to the infant's entire future life is the way she cares for him. Yet she is offered little concrete help or information in the dynamics of infant psychology, due to the naive assumption that good mothering ability comes naturally to women, and especially to new mothers.

Mother is often blamed for her children's failures in later life. If she lives for her children she is "overprotective," to their ruination. If she pursues a life of her own she is "neglectful," with the same result. If, when her children are grown, she pursues the volunteer interests open to her she becomes a figure of fun, a cartoon club-lady. If she pursues or revives a second career in later life, she is seldom taken seriously (and probably is accused of neglecting her husband as well). Society continues to let little girls know that the justification for women is that they are needed to be mothers. But everywhere except on Christmas and Mother's Day cards, "mother" is treated as a bad and sometimes vicious joke.

From infancy, both men and women have misgivings about women that are rooted in their ambivalence about mother. In addition to this, however, the boy child as he grows discovers new exasperations about women which tend to confirm his earlier suspicions about them. He discovers that girls are allowed to cry while he is not, and that they are allowed to run away from danger rather than being obliged to "face it like a man." Most infuriating of all, girls are permitted to tease him, but under no circumstances is he allowed to retaliate in the only way he knows—by hitting them. Many a man recalls suppressing his rage when he was told as a boy, "I don't care what she did, boys do not hit girls." As a result of such experiences, by the time he reaches his teens the average American boy is not well-disposed toward women.

MANHOOD MUST BE WON

There is another possible reason why men grow up to dislike women. While men and women share the struggle to come to terms with mother, men alone must face a related struggle—the widely discussed fragility of the male ego and how to live with it.

Margaret Mead has suggested, not entirely facetiously, that the architect of man's ego is woman and that she has designed it for her own purposes. Dr. Mead tells a story of a society of primitive people who live near a snake- and crocodile-infested swamp and who depend for their food on what they can hunt there. She postulates, sensibly enough, that nobody, male or female, enjoys venturing into the swamp with all its terrors, but that in order to maintain the group and feed the children someone must do so. Women, being always concerned about the welfare of the children, have stumbled upon an ingenious method for getting food from the swamp without risking a trip there themselves. Somehow, according to this scenario, the women have figured out that they can get the men to go by flattering them about their courage and then taunting them about their lack of "manliness" when they balk at proving that courage on the hunt. In time, the women establish a pattern of developing fragile and easily wounded egos in their sons so that they can shame them into doing the necessary but distinctly unpleasant task of providing for a family.[5]

Intriguing as this scheme is, Dr. Mead does not upon sober reflection assert that women have been either clever or diabolical enough to deliberately attempt to control men in this way. Yet every woman knows from girlhood that men are easily-hurt, proud creatures who must be treated with the greatest tact and delicacy. If not a feminine conspiracy, what is behind this fragile pride that will cause a man to fight when common sense says he should run?

H. R. Hays, in summing up his entertaining survey of misogyny through the ages, *The Dangerous Sex*, makes a point that others often skirt, namely that man's insecurity about his relationship with woman has its root in his nagging insecurity about his ability to perform sexually.

All the material we have been discussing indicates that men have always been fragile in their sex life. Women can fulfill their sexual role in society without effort, by mere acceptance; their need for orgasmic experience has varied with the culture's expectations. Men, however, must be capable of erection and discharge or they are not performing their duty in carrying on the race. . . . Thus men have worried about their potency from the beginning of history. . . .[6]

The notebooks of analysts are filled with cases of men whose anxiety about real or imagined impotence has caused them deep distress. The pain of adolescence for boys is tied up with the struggle for self-respect in manhood. Sexual experimentation becomes central at this time because a young man's feeling of self-worth and the respect of his peers are closely related to his sexual prowess.

A man's ability to perform sexually becomes crucial to his self-esteem. Though women too can fail to achieve sexual satisfaction, they can pretend to have done so. Man's failure is both involuntary and obvious, a source of humiliation. Worst of all, woman is witness to his failure.

SILENCING THE WITNESS

To be humiliated in the presence of a peer is far more painful than to have an inferior see you at your worst. Hence, if woman can be kept in a state of subjugation that is acknowledged by everyone, sexual failure in her presence is less important. If woman is man's inferior or subordinate she has no cause to complain of his failure. Even a failed man is more than a woman.

Another way to deal with humiliation is to blame it on someone else. We can all recall occasions when in bitter disappointment we have discovered reasons outside ourselves (and usually in other people) for our failures. The classical biblical example of this is Adam's lame excuse: "the woman whom thou gavest to be with me" (your fault, God) "she gave me the fruit of the tree" (her fault) "and I did eat" (naturally).[7]

When man fails sexually the easiest way to handle it is to blame the only other person involved. If she were more skilled in the art of love, if she were more attractive, if she were more responsive, everything would be all right. ("Want him to be more of a man? Try being more of a woman.")

The message that man's sexual failure is woman's problem and not his is all around us. It's not that men are impotent, it's that women are frigid. When woman begins to accept the responsibility for man's sexual prowess, she takes on his insecurity and anxiety about sex and makes them her own.

SEX AND RELIGION

But even if we acknowledge man's sexual insecurity, what does it have to do with our subject, women in the priesthood? Curiously enough, some of the arguments advanced for keeping women out of the priesthood deal with exactly the dynamics we have been discussing. It is strongly implied by some that since man properly takes the initiative in the sex act only male priests may take initiative in the life of the church.[8] We also find that the New Testament image of the church as the bride of Christ is used to justify an all-male clergy, apparently on the assumption that the priest represents Christ and the laity his bride.[9]

Humankind's two most basic needs are to be fed and to be loved. Religions throughout the world and throughout history have centered on ritual feeding or ritual love-making, sometimes combining the two. That the need to be loved and the need to be fed are deep and interrelated can readily be drawn from the experience of any of us, and reminds us again of our earlier discussion of that lost paradise of mother love. It is little wonder then that our Christian sacrament of feeding becomes so conflated with our need to be loved that sexual considerations are seen as important to the proper performance of sacramental acts.

The Eucharist is not a sexual sacrament. It is a sacrament of feeding. All humans of whatever age or condition share the need to be fed. Though there are people who do not engage in sexual activity, no one lives who does not eat. Hence the sacramental bread and wine recall for Christians how basic are God's gifts to our very existence. We give thanks that we continue to be fed, both physically and spiritually.

MANHOOD AND THE WORLD OF WORK

There are still other possible explanations of man's dread of woman as it manifests itself in his reluctance to have her join him as a peer in the world of work. The possibility that men envy women their ability to create life itself has often been cited to explain male genius in the arts and sciences and female lack of such genius. We are told that men compensate for their inability to give birth by writing symphonies and building cathedrals, and there may well be some truth in that assertion. The corollary is that women are not geniuses because they don't have to be. What edifice or poem could rival a new-born infant?

As long as women create babies and men create everything else, our world, if not perfect, appears at least to be balanced. However, when women decide that they would like to exercise their abilities in a variety of ways, the system of compensations is altered and men feel threatened. Women should stick to their own realm and give birth. It is simply not fair that they should want to compete with men as well. Men do not attempt to compete with women as mothers, why should women be permitted to compete with men as artists and writers?

Increasingly, our society is coming to recognize that talent and ability are not sex-linked. Furthermore, we are living in a time when pregnancy and motherhood need not be involuntary and can in most cases be freely chosen. Large families, rather than being desperately needed as in past ages, are beginning to be viewed as an ecological liability. The logic of all these factors is that women should now be free to share the tasks and joys of all kinds of work.

However, women who aspire to use their talents in pursuits other than motherhood run into masculine resentment. It's not fair that women can function in two realms, motherhood and work, and men cannot. In addition, woman's encroachment on man's territory infringes on his first defense against sexual impotence—his failure in sex is minimized as long as he remains superior to woman in other realms. Again in Hays's view: "The man in a highly developed society equates his work and his achievement with his potency. . . . Women not only make frightening physical demands upon him . . . but castrate him creatively by possibly doing his work better." [10]

MANHOOD AND PRIESTHOOD

Clergy have a special problem in admitting women to their profession. In our society many of the things that priests do and the manner in which they are done connote femininity.

Margaretta K. Bowers, an American psychiatrist and Episcopal laywoman who specializes in treating clergy and especially Episcopal priests, points this out clearly in relation to clerical fondness for vestments and ceremony:

> There is a definite insistence in our culture that the enjoyment of walking in the rustlings of silk and satins, lace petticoats, and magnificent cloth of gold, is an expression of femininity. The fact that men throughout the ages, throughout the world, have enjoyed these luxuries and considered them masculine, seems to have little weight in the argument. In our culture, a man in a cassock is wearing a skirt, and therefore is getting away with something which he could not do in civilian clothes. There is a certain pleasure in the flaunting of a special privilege; there is a special conceit in doing what the ordinary man cannot do.[11]

If there is a special privilege, there is also a special danger that the man in the cassock/skirt will be seen as effeminate. As long as it is axiomatic that priests may do these things because they are priests and that women are never priests, the specter of effeminacy does not rise. But once women become priests it will be clear to all that many of the duties of a priest are duties which this society happens to consider as belonging in woman's realm.

When a woman dons vestments we suddenly recognize that in this society they resemble more what women wear than they do the garb of men. (Historically, of course, they are the everyday dress of males of another age.) When a woman breaks bread and serves wine, then cleans the vessels when all have been fed, we suddenly recognize that she has served a meal and done the dishes, just as women do at home. When a woman hears confession or gives absolution we recognize that women are the listeners and comforters at home, too.

The world in which many clergy move is also a feminine world. Women outnumber men in church not only on Sunday but throughout the week as well. The suburban communities in which many clergy work are also predominantly female during weekday business hours. As long as his very costume (the clerical collar) assures him that he is a man, the priest can move freely and without embarrassment in these women's worlds. But once women start wearing that costume and doing his work, doubts and questions about the "manliness" of his profession may arise.

"DIFFERENCE" AND THE GOSPEL

Woman is seen as "different" and therefore unsuited to priesthood for a host of reasons. The most important of these is that man does not choose to see her otherwise. He is, at a deep level of his being, fearful of woman and has constructed an elaborate system of defenses to keep her at bay.

As Christians we are bound to ask seriously whether woman's "difference" is part of God's revelation and the divine order, or whether it is an accommodation to male ambivalence. If it is the former, Christians should deplore the changing role of women in society and reject any thought of women clergy. If it is the latter, Christians should be in the forefront of the people working to shape a new life for both women and men based on their common humanity.

CHAPTER
5

ADAM'S
RIB

Unexamined emotions and preconceptions concerning women have hindered the church from taking the possibility of woman's vocation to the priesthood seriously enough to give it detailed theological study until recently. The mind-set which prevented earlier attention to the question is illustrated by the words of the "father of Anglican theologians," Richard Hooker. Hooker states his estimate of women in his book *The Ecclesiastical Polity* when, in the course of an argument for maintaining the custom of "giving away" the bride in the marriage ceremony, he declares, "It putteth women in mind of a duty whereunto the very imbecility of their nature and sex doth bind them; namely, to be always directed, guided, and ordered by others." [1]

Today, such an assertion would be an embarrassment to an opponent of women in the priesthood. Theological statements are usually careful to avoid suggesting that women are inferior creatures. In a recent article, the Rt. Rev. C. Kilmer Myers vigorously opposes the ordination of women to the priesthood, but insists, "This is *not* an assertion of male superiority." [2] Modern opponents of women in the priesthood claim not that women are inferior, but that they are different. A perennially popular English pamphlet opposing women in the priesthood puts it this way:

Any element of subordination, in the strict sense of that word, which is involved carries with it no suggestion of inferiority but only one of difference between the sexes, a difference which is manifested no less in the fact that a woman was chosen to be the Mother of God than in the fact that the Second Person of the Ever-blessed Trinity became man in our nature as her son.[3]

We will put off until the next chapter an examination of the second part of this passage, that is, the implications of masculine and feminine biblical images for the ordination of women to the priesthood. What we want to focus on in this chapter is that "element of subordination" which connotes "no suggestion of inferiority." This elusive concept often appears in arguments against the ordination of women to the priesthood. Perhaps the essence of the argument was captured by the priest who said, "Woman cannot be a priest, because she is equal but beneath man." [4]

SUBORDINATION

The notion that women are subordinate to men occupies a special position in the arsenal of biblical and theological arguments against the ordination of women to the priesthood. It is the *only* theological argument against the priesting of women that is also used in the New Testament to limit the role of women in the life of the church. When Paul and other New Testament writers place limits on women's behavior in the early Christian congregations, they use this argument alone as a theological justification. It should be emphasized as well that the New Testament writers do not direct special arguments against women in Holy Orders or women priests. Nor do they extend restrictions to women in the church which exceed the restrictions placed upon women in other areas of social life.[5]

Two New Testament passages governing the proper role of women in the church have long served as the basis for the doctrine of the subordination of women to men. Both occur in Paul's first epistle to the Corinthians, and the passages derive much of their authority from their location in a document of undisputed Pauline authorship.[6] The Revised Standard Version of the Bible renders the two passages as follows:

I commend you because you remember me in everything and maintain the traditions even as I have delivered them to you. But I want you to understand that the head of every man is Christ, the head of a woman is her husband, and the head of Christ is God. Any man who prays or prophesies with his head covered dishonors his head, but any woman who prays or prophesies with her head unveiled dishonors her head—it is the same as if her head were shaven. For if a woman will not veil herself, then she should cut off her hair; but if it is disgraceful for a woman to be shorn or shaven, let her wear a veil. For a man ought not to cover his head, since he is the image and glory of God; but woman is the glory of man. (For man was not made from woman, but woman from man. Neither was man created for woman, but woman for man.)—1 Corinthians 11:2–9

As in all the churches of the saints, the women should keep silence in the churches. For they are not permitted to speak, but should be subordinate, as even the law says. If there is anything they desire to know, let them ask their husbands at home. For it is shameful for a woman to speak in church.—1 Corinthians 14:33–35

On an initial inspection of these texts, our response must be confusion. In 1 Corinthians 14:34, Paul is urging silence on all women in the churches, yet in 11:4–5, he seems to assume that women will pray and prophesy in public church gatherings and merely seeks to regulate the matter of women's dress—that they should be veiled. There have been ingenious efforts to sort out and explain the apparent inconsistencies here, but they need not detain us because the two passages are in agreement on the crucial point: women are subordinate to men.

Paul's view of women's subordination to men is stated in verses 3 and 7–9 of 1 Corinthians 11 and in verse 34 of 1 Corinthians 14. In chapter 11, it is clear that Paul is thinking of the creation narratives in Genesis 1 and 2 as a basis for his view of the subordinate role of women. In chapter 14, he refers in a general way to "the law" as his authority. Commentators generally suggest that he is referring here to Genesis 3:16, which tells the consequences of the fall for woman and reads, in part, "your desire shall be for your husband and he shall rule over you." [7]

1 Corinthians 11 and 14 combine both pastoral advice ("behave this way") with theological interpretation ("because Genesis says so"). A contemporary interpretation of these passages must consider both aspects—the relevance of Paul's pastoral advice for today's church and the soundness of the theological position he adopts to support his advice.[8]

PASTORAL ADVICE: DECENTLY AND IN ORDER

Paul was faced with the task of helping a rather unpopular new religious movement flourish and grow. This meant that there had to be limits on the extent to which the church could encourage a life-style different from the customary behavior of the day. Despite Paul's efforts to see that everything in the churches was done "decently and in order" (1 Corinthians 14:40), the early Christians were in constant danger of being thought subversive in the area of family relations. The new sect encouraged membership and participation of women in a way that was unknown in the Jewish synagogue; this innovation threatened to undermine traditional man-woman relationships, especially in marriage. It is no accident that both 1 Corinthians 11 and 1 Corinthians 14 appear to deal with the man-woman relationship in marriage. The marriage relationship was closely regulated

by custom and, as most adult women were married, it would
be their conduct that caused Paul special concern.

Rigid social conventions regulated the conduct of women
in the first-century Hellenistic world. Wives were regarded
in both Palestine and Greece as the property of their husbands, and they were expected to observe social conventions
faithfully in order to avoid bringing dishonor on their
husbands. A woman needed to exercise particular care that
she not give the appearance of being an adulteress or a
prostitute. To protect herself and her husband from scandal,
she exercised discretion in appearance and speech. She
neither spoke in public, nor appeared outside her home un-
less covered with a veil.[9]

Given this context, what is surprising is not that women
did so little in the early Christian congregations such as
Corinth, but that they evidently had freedom to do so
much. They gathered together with men in public church
meetings and apparently prayed and prophesied from time
to time. Their participation in the Christian congregations
exceeded the usual limits of woman's role in the first-century Hellenistic world, doubtless more than once to the
point of scandal. It was in this setting that Paul urged the
women of Corinth to "wear a veil" and to "keep silence."

Today, the pastoral guidelines which Paul laid down for
proper behavior in 1 Corinthians 11 and 14 are more honored in the breach than the observance. Episcopalians have
long since decided that Paul's suggestions on dress and
decorum—however helpful for maintaining the church in
the first century—do not apply in different circumstances.
It is no longer unthinkable for a woman to appear in church
without covering her head. Men—particularly clergy—occasionally attend services wearing head coverings (the
bishop's mitre, for instance) in direct contravention of 1
Corinthians 11:7.

It is also common for women—both in this country and

in Anglican churches abroad—to take a vocal role in all kinds of public church gatherings, as vestry members, speakers, teachers, or convention delegates. In fact, the role of women in conventions should probably be seen as the most blatant violation of Paul's directions. The wide publicity accorded such gatherings makes a woman's participation there much more of a scandal, in Paul's terms, than her leadership at the services of a local church would be.

THEOLOGICAL ADVICE: BE SUBORDINATE

Opponents of the ordination of women to the priesthood are willing to brave charges of inconsistency to maintain that whatever else women may now do in the churches, Paul's words rule out their priesthood. In this one area, at least, the principle of subordination still applies. Changing social conventions may have opened other areas of the church's life to women, but in the central institution of the priesthood, the theological principle of subordination applies. It is precisely this "theological principle" which we will now examine.

1 CORINTHIANS 11:7-9

In 1 Corinthians 11:7 Paul has pulled together the two different creation stories from Genesis 1 and 2 and conflated them into an argument for the veiling of women: "For a man ought not to cover his head, since he is the image and glory of God; but woman is the glory of man." However, when we read Genesis 1 and 2 to see where Paul got this idea, we see that his interpretation is a distortion of the two creation stories.

The two creation stories go this way. In Genesis 1:27 we read that "God created man in his own image, in the image

of God he created him; male and female he created them."
In the account in Genesis 2, God creates Adam first from
"dust of the ground" (v. 7) and later forms Eve from
Adam's rib to be "a helper fit for him" (vv. 18–22). In the
Genesis 1 account, both man and woman are formed in the
image of God. In the Genesis 2 version, neither man nor
woman is formed in God's image. Adam is made from dust
and Eve is made from Adam's rib, but the story doesn't
mention that either of them is made in God's image.

Now what Paul said was that "man . . . is the image
and glory of God; but woman is the glory of man"—a
statement that strongly suggests that man is made in God's
image and woman is not. But if this is what Paul meant, he
has misread his proof-texts, because neither Genesis 1 nor
Genesis 2 will support him. The subordination of women to
men cannot be argued on the basis that one sex (male) is
made in God's image while the other sex (female) is not.

In 1 Corinthians 11:8–9, Paul focuses on the Genesis 2
creation story in an effort to reinforce his point: "For man
was not made from woman, but woman from man. Neither
was man created for woman, but woman for man." In this
argument Paul takes the fact that Eve was created after
Adam in order to be a "helper fit for him" and uses it to
suggest that women should observe their proper, subordinate
role. Does it follow from the story of the creation of Eve
from Adam's rib that she is therefore Adam's subordinate?

We can investigate this question by looking at the language which the author of Genesis 2 uses to describe Eve's
role. We are told that she is to be a "helper" to Adam. Even
with the qualification "fit for him," the term "helper" connotes inferiority in English, perhaps an assistant. At worst,
the term suggests that Eve is to be Adam's housekeeper, or
perhaps his maidservant. But the Hebrew word *ezer*, which
is here translated "helper," carries no such connotation of
inferiority in other places where it is used in the Old Testa-

ment. As a summary of a study of the use of *ezer* in the Old
Testament concludes:

> It is used twenty-one times in the Old Testament, and sixteen
> times it is used for a super-ordinate, not a subordinate, helper. In
> no case is the one who helps subordinate unless we consider
> Genesis 2:18, 20 as exceptions. The most common use of *ezer*
> is in reference to Jehovah as a help. In Psalm 33:20 we read:
> "The Lord, He is our help." Exodus 18:4, "For the God of my
> father was my help." Psalm 146:5, "Happy is he that hath the
> God of Jacob for his help." If this word *ezer*, "help," does in-
> dicate a grade or rank, we should conclude from its use elsewhere
> in the Old Testament that Adam was subordinate to Eve. The
> truth is that the word itself indicates neither a higher nor a
> lower grade or rank.[10]

It is extremely unlikely that the author of Genesis 2 intended to convey the idea that Eve was Adam's inferior by
describing her as Adam's helper. Despite the fact that the
passage has often been interpreted this way, from Paul's
day to our own, it cannot be used as evidence for woman's
inferior or subordinate place in the created order.

1 CORINTHIANS 14:34

In 1 Corinthians 14:34, Paul invokes another Genesis passage, the story of the fall, to argue that women should oc-
cupy a subordinate place in church life. According to
Genesis 3:16, one of the consequences of the fall was that
woman would be ruled by her husband. Paul's statement
that women "should be subordinate, as even the law says"
is certainly a legitimate interpretation of the results of the
fall for the man-woman relationship in marriage.

   However, the question we are faced with today is whether
the man-woman relations that resulted from the fall are
appropriate in the Christian community. Is it still true that
women are subordinate to their husbands as they have been

since they left the Garden of Eden? This is a central issue and one about which the New Testament itself gives conflicting opinions. The same Paul who instructs women to be "subordinate, as even the law says," also tells us (in 1 Corinthians 11:11–12) that "in the Lord woman is not independent of man nor man of woman; for as woman was made from man, so man is now born of woman. And all things are from God." In Galatians 3:28, Paul asserts, "There is neither Jew nor Greek, there is neither slave nor free, there is neither male nor female; for you are all one in Christ Jesus."

TWO VIEWS OF MAN-WOMAN RELATIONS

The New Testament, then, outlines two types of man-woman relationships—those which obtain under the law (1 Corinthians 14:34) and those which exist "in Christ" (Galatians 3:28). These two approaches existed in tension in St. Paul's thought and are both recorded in Scripture. The problem for the contemporary reader is deciding which of the two approaches best embodies the central message of the Gospel, in order to find a guideline for man-woman relationships today.

Opponents of women in the priesthood are not, by and large, willing to take this problem seriously. They would like to "have it both ways." They would like to accept *both* the message of a new man-woman relation "in Christ" and the message that women are subordinate, "as even the law says." Their way out of this dilemma is sometimes to suggest that the message of Galatians 3:28 does not apply to life in this world, but only to life "at the end of time." They would argue that yes, we are all equal before God, but in this age we are still bound by the conditions that resulted from the fall. One writer dismisses the Galatians passage this way: "[Paul's] remark is clearly intended as eschato-

logical—having to do with 'the last days'—when 'God will
be all in all.' In other words, the Galatians passage is irrelevant to the issue under discussion." [11] The author goes
on to challenge those who want the priesthood opened to
women to state their criteria for preferring the Galatians
passage to 1 Corinthians 14:34 as a guideline for the
churches today.[12]

Before picking up that challenge, we should examine the
implications of saying that the Galatians passage is "irrelevant" because it points only to "the last days." To say
that the Galatians passage is irrelevant is to say that all
efforts to break down the barriers of enmity that exist between different groups are inappropriate to this age. This
would mean that the church would never seek to erase in
its own life those distinctions which flow from race and
ethnicity, condition of servitude, or sex. This is plainly re-
pugnant and no opponent of the ordination of women to
the priesthood that we know of advances such a position.
However, such a position ought to be the logical conse-
quence of an interpretation that views Galatians 3:28 as
"irrelevant."

In a similar vein, others argue that, if the Galatians passage were intended for implementation in the life of the
church, it would have been implemented in apostolic times
and we would see the results of this in the New Testament.[13] This effort to play what Krister Stendahl has called
"First-Century Bible Land" [14]—to try to maintain in our
churches the relations which obtained between different
groups at the time the New Testament was composed—
leads to contradictions as well. We would then—following
the New Testament practice—regard the emancipation of
slaves as contrary to God's will for us, and would try to
maintain in the church some reminders that slaves are not
free in this world (perhaps descendants of slaves could sit
at the back of the church, or be employed by the church in

those jobs formerly performed by slaves). Fortunately, no opponent of the priesting of women that we know of has suggested such a desperate expedient.

GALATIANS 3:28

In fact, there are good interpretive principles for preferring Galatians 3:28 to 1 Corinthians 14:34 as the embodiment of the central message of the Gospel.

In the first place, Galatians 3:28 is found in a theological discourse in which Paul is discussing the saving work of Christ. 1 Corinthians 14:34, on the other hand, is incorporated in a set of practical directions for maintaining church order. Between the two, we should probably assume that the passage which is basically "theological" in character has more long-term importance and relevance for the church.[15]

In fact, Galatians 3:28 has special theological importance because it is describing the order of things in the kingdom, "in Christ." [16] As Christians we live between two worlds, between this world and the Kingdom of God. This world, as much as we seem to be bound up in it, is not where we "live and move and have our being." Our real life as Christians is "in Christ." When we pray the Lord's Prayer, we say, "Our Father, who art in heaven, Hallowed be thy Name. Thy kingdom come. Thy will be done, On earth as it is in heaven." We ask that God work to establish the order of the kingdom on earth, here and now.[17] We do not ask God to put off his saving work until some "last days" that are always at the other end of the rainbow. We do not know exactly what God's kingdom will be like, but the New Testament gives us some glimpses and one of those glimpses is in Galatians 3:28. We know about the kingdom through our life "in Christ." And "in Christ" there is "neither Jew nor Greek, there is neither slave nor free, there is neither male nor female."

The theological importance of the Galatians passage is underscored by the fact that it speaks of a new order which reverses the effects of the fall.[18] In Romans 5:18 Paul says, "Then as one man's trespass led to condemnation for all men, so one man's act of righteousness leads to acquittal and life for all men." The subordination of women to men was one of the effects of the fall, as we know from Genesis 3:16. In Christ's death and resurrection we are freed from bondage to the sinful conditions of existence that obtained under the fall. If Paul had never written Galatians 3:28, we would be compelled to affirm its principles on the basis of what we know of Christ's work from the rest of the New Testament.

If we accept Galatians 3:28 as consistent with the central message of the New Testament, we must discard the theological doctrine of subordination which St. Paul uses in 1 Corinthians 11 and 14 to justify his pastoral concern that the Christian churches conduct themselves "decently and in order." At the same time, we should be alerted to the limitations of other images Paul employs to describe man-woman relations. The notion of subordination that is implied in 1 Corinthians 11:3 ("But I want you to understand that the head of every man is Christ, the head of a woman is her husband, and the head of Christ is God") is likewise inconsistent with the kingdom order proclaimed in Galatians 3:28. A man might be the "head" of his wife under the conditions of the fall, but not in Christ.[19]

CHAPTER
6

ANATOMY
AND
MINISTRY

In the preceding chapter we examined and rejected the argument that women should be subordinate to men in our life together in Christ. We consider here the second type of theological argument advanced against women in the priesthood—that God intends women and men to fill separate roles in the life of Christ's church. The unhappy history of the "separate but equal" doctrine in certain branches of our civil life has been no deterrent to its use in various guises by those who oppose the ordination of women priests:

If women are incapable of receiving Holy Orders, it cannot be just because they are, in the vulgar sense of the word, *subordinate* to men, but because of the particular way in which masculinity and femininity are involved in the whole dispensation of redemption.[1]

According to opponents of women in the priesthood, there are different spheres for the ministry of men and women. These are defined by biblical imagery and biblical and traditional precedents. An all-male priesthood is dictated by the fact that the priest is a God-symbol and God has traditionally been represented through male imagery. Likewise, the priest is a representative of Christ, who was incarnate as a male. No woman can represent Christ to God's people. Not only was Jesus male, but so also were his chosen followers, the Twelve. If Jesus had intended women to minister as priests in his name, surely he would have selected women to be among the Twelve Disciples.

The model for women's ministry, the argument proceeds, may be seen in the life and witness of Mary, the mother of Jesus. Women are blessed with a special ministry in motherhood and the home which precludes their assuming priestly functions. Some or all of these points are frequently gathered together as a basis for asserting that the priesting of women would be against the will of God for his church.

Before we take up each of these arguments in turn, we should recall that New Testament writers never suggest that the proper place of women in the church is determined by the masculinity of God or the fact that Jesus and the Twelve were male. As Stendahl points out: "In all of the texts where the New Testament speaks about the role of women in the church, we have found that when a reason is given, it is always by reference to the subordinate position of woman in the order of creation." [2]

GOD THE FATHER

Opponents of women in the priesthood argue that the priest must function as a God-symbol in the church. Women are disqualified from serving as priests because they do not embody certain qualities which are associated with members of the male sex. Albert J. duBois, writing in *The Episcopalian*, phrases the argument this way:

The male has the initiative in creation. The act of blessing, which is the fundamental priestly act, is creative. To say "Bless us" is the supplicatory prerogative of any minister, but to stretch out a hand and say "Bless this" is to initiate a creation. In this the male priest reflects the creative activity of God the Father.[3]

A similar point is made by the Rt. Rev. C. Kilmer Myers:

A priest is a "God-symbol" whether he likes it or not. In the imagery of both the Old and New Testaments God is represented in masculine imagery. The Father begets the Son. This is essential to the *givingness* of the Christian Faith, and to tamper with this imagery is to change that Faith into something else.

Of course, this does not mean God is a male. The biblical language is the language of analogy. It is imperfect, even as all human imagery of God must be imperfect. Nevertheless, it has meaning. The male image about God pertains to the divine initiative in creation. Initiative is, in itself, a male rather than a female attribute.[4]

It is no easy matter to sort out precisely what is being asserted by these writers (with the exception of Myers' point that God is represented in Scripture through masculine imagery). But surely this much is claimed: (1) God's work as creator of all is an exercise of masculine initiative; and (2) a priest's exercise of male initiative in the sacramental acts is analogous to God's creative activity. Let us examine these claims. We will return later to the question of the masculine scriptural imagery of God.

Both writers assume that God acts in a "male" capacity as creator of all things. But despite the masculine biblical imagery, Christians must assert that God cannot be comprehended and classified by the language with which we speak of him. This point has been made by another opponent of the ordination of women priests:

. . . our objection to the ordination of women to the priesthood (and the episcopate) is not rooted in our doctrine of God. We do not argue that God is masculine, and it is an axiom in Christian theology that God is without sex, or, more accurately, that he comprehends within the mystery of his being *all* the positive values of sexuality—masculine, feminine, or whatever —and that to a degree beyond human imagining.[5]

Anglicans especially should be warned against a view of God as "male" or "masculine." The first of the Anglican Articles of Religion (which have served since the sixteenth century as useful touchstones in matters of doctrine) explicitly denies that God can be reduced to the images we usually employ in speaking of him: "There is but one living and true God, everlasting, without body, parts, or passions. . . ." [6] We must be careful not to allow the limits of our language to carry us along to a crude anthropomorphism. It verges on anthropomorphism to suggest that God's "male" character is evident in some designated sphere of his activity.

Both the above-quoted writers also assume that the priest exercises masculine initiative or creativity in a manner analogous to God's creative, initiating capacity as Father of all. Both writers believe that men are able to act in the image of God in a creative, initiating role that women are unable to fill. The assumption that men and men only are able to act in a creative, initiating role does not hold up well in a world that knows women artists and heads-of-state. But there is another difficulty with this notion. There is a theological difficulty with the claim that *either* man or woman can show forth God's initiating, creative capacity. In his commentary on Genesis 1:26, Alan Richardson, Dean of York, says:

It has become the fashion in certain quarters to assert that God's likeness in man is most clearly perceived in the fact that man shares in God's creativity; we hear much about man's "creative" powers, as artists, craftsmen, scientists, and so on. The *imago Dei* is made to consist in man's capacity for creative activity. This is not what the Bible teaches. It is clear that [the author of Genesis 1:26] thinks of the likeness of God in man as manifest in man's sharing in the Creator's *dominium* over the rest of the created order, especially over the animal world. [7]

The word "man" used in Richardson's passage refers, of course, to man created in the image of God, male and female: "Let them [male and female] have dominion. . . ." Neither men nor women may be compared to God as creator. Our role—and it is a role that men and women share—is the exercise of God-given authority over the rest of creation. There is no basis for the theological argument that "the male priest reflects the creative activity of God the Father." The image of God is reflected in neither men nor women in this way.

However serious the theological difficulties inherent in analogies between God the Father and male priests, there is no doubt that most of the biblical imagery of God is masculine. Such imagery is not "invariably" masculine as is sometimes claimed, however.[8]

In Luke 15, we find one of the best-known series of Jesus' parables. Jesus uses three stories to help his followers understand the will of God: the parables of the lost sheep, the lost coin, and the prodigal son. In each of these stories one of the characters represents God. In the parables of the lost sheep and the prodigal son, the God-figure is a man, but in the parable of the lost coin, the God-figure is a woman.[9] Jesus also uses maternal imagery to describe his own relationship to his people: "O Jerusalem, Jerusalem, killing the prophets and stoning those who are sent to you! How often would I have gathered your children together as a hen gathers her brood under her wings, and you would not!" (Luke 13:34).

Remarkable as it may seem, the predominantly masculine imagery used to describe God, from the days of Ancient Israel to our own, has not prevented God from calling women to represent him before his people. Both Israel and the early Christian communities knew and honored women among their prophets. Prophets are recognized as representatives of God among his people.

JESUS AND THE TWELVE

It is often asserted that women must be excluded from the priesthood of the church because God became incarnate in a male person—Jesus of Nazareth. Proponents of the view recognize that the incarnation involves the "scandal of particularity"—that the saviour of the whole world became flesh under specific conditions of race, religion, time, economic status, and sex. It is understood that Jesus could not have existed in history and belonged at the same time to every social group; God particularizes in order to universalize. At this point in the discussion, opponents of the ordination of women to the priesthood assert that though other particularities of Jesus' historical existence were accidental, his sex has special significance:

> Being a Jew, being a Palestinian, being a first-century man— all these are what we might call, in the language of Aristotelian metaphysics, the "accidents" of Christ's humanity; but his being a man rather than a woman is of the "substance" of his humanity. He could have been a twentieth-century Chinese and been, cultural differences notwithstanding, much the same person he was; but he could not have been a woman without having been a different sort of personality altogether.[10]

The importance of Jesus' sex is underscored by the fact that he chose for his official followers twelve men—a precedent for the traditionally male priesthood of the church.[11]

These arguments appear to take seriously the historical circumstances of the incarnation, but in fact, by their overemphasis on the sex of Jesus and the Twelve, they leave much out of account. We should take seriously the fact that Jesus' earthly ministry occurred in continuity with God's work for and among the people of Israel. Jesus, Christians believe, was the Messiah anticipated by the Jews. If we see Jesus in this way, we will take seriously not only his maleness, but also his Jewishness, his Davidic ancestry, and his status as freeman rather than slave. We will regard all these attributes of his person not as "accidents" but as attributes of theological significance.

The theological significance of these attributes—male, Jewish, free, of Davidic descent—lies in the fact that God's saving work in Christ is also seen by Christians as the fulfillment of God's promises to the people of Israel. Jesus both fulfilled the law and the prophets and initiated a new age in the relations between God and his people. The Messiah was to be David's royal son: a Jewish male, freeman. Gentiles held no theological status in Israel, and the position of slaves and women, although it varied somewhat during the history of Israel, was never equal to that of men. Only a man could fulfill the expectations of the Old Testament. As Leonard Hodgson puts it:

[Jesus'] earthly life was lived within the circle of the Jewish religious thought of His time. He had come as Messiah to be offered in sacrifice as the Lamb of God for the taking away of the sins of the world. For this a male without blemish was required by Jewish law.[12]

The appointment of the Twelve should also be looked at in the context of Jewish religious thought of the first century. The Twelve are symbolic of the twelve tribes of Israel and serve as the fulfillment of the prophecy of the restoration of Israel. Jesus gathered the Twelve in fulfillment of the prophecy that the heir to David's throne would bring back together the scattered tribes of Israel. According to Jewish theology, the representatives of the twelve tribes would, of necessity, be Jewish freemen.[13]

The significance not only of the sex, but also of the race and number of the disciples, is further suggested by Urban Holmes in his recent book *The Future Shape of Ministry*:

. . . the fact that Jesus did appoint the Twelve (which is probably a historically accurate record) would have nothing to do with the establishment of an institutional Church as we know it, but would be an eschatological sign in anticipation of the fulfillment of Israel in the Kingdom that was about to come, the Twelve not functioning as apostles (Matt. 19:28; Luke 22:30) but symbolizing the Twelve Tribes of Israel on the Day of the Lord.[14]

THE NEW ISRAEL

The personal characteristics of Jesus and the Twelve are not insignificant. They are theologically significant for the fulfillment of the messianic prophecies made under the old covenant between God and his people Israel. But they are not therefore determinative for our ministry in the New Israel, which came into being after the resurrection. Holmes urges caution in seeking models for ministry in particular elements of Jesus' earthly ministry:

. . . we should be careful about any arguments concerning the nature of the Church and the function of the ministry derived from the historical Jesus. It is with the Resurrection event that the whole question becomes alive. For Paul and Peter as well as ourselves it is the central reality of our Christian faith. Jesus is raised and glorified, he is the "first fruits" of what we are and are not yet; and we are sent to make known the mystery of his person throughout the world until all be fulfilled in him.[15]

The implications of Jesus' death and resurrection were not immediately apparent to his followers. It took time for them to understand that the Gospel was for Gentiles as well as for Jews. The controversy between those who saw Christianity as a Jewish sect, open only to the circumcised, and those like Paul, who insisted that salvation in Christ was for all people, echoes throughout the Book of Acts and the Epistles. Acts 10 tells how Peter came to realize that Christ's saving work extended to Gentiles. Peter was in the home of Cornelius, a centurion in Caesarea, and was astounded to see that Cornelius and other Gentiles who were with him received the ecstatic gifts of the Holy Spirit. "Can anyone forbid water for baptizing these people who have received the Holy Spirit just as we have?" he asked (Acts 10:47).

At length it became clear to the early Christians that in the New Israel the old theological distinctions between Jew and Gentile, slave and free, male and female, were broken down. Membership in the body of Christ was open to all people, irrespective of the divisions that had existed under Jewish law. It is then no less a sign of the reconciling work of Christ that Gentile men can minister as priests in his name than it would be for women to do so. The ministries of both groups flow from the universal nature of God's saving work in Christ and the universal mission of his church.

MOTHERHOOD AND MINISTRY

Opponents of women in the priesthood urge the Christian woman to follow Christ, but by a particular route. She has distinctive functions in building Christ's kingdom and she should look to Mary, the mother of Jesus, and other prominent Bible women for models for her life. Above all, her role in building the kingdom is associated with her ministry as Christian wife and mother.

According to one opponent of the ordination of women to the priesthood, woman's role flows directly from her biological potential for motherhood:

The femininity of woman is clearly marked out by her bodily functions. By nature she is destined for a different life from the man's. However much she tries to avoid this (and the modern methods of avoiding it are many and full of dangers), she can never really escape it. For every normal woman is a potential mother. . . .[16]

By contrast, the same writer states, "every man . . . is a potential priest." [17]

The implications of woman's role as Christian wife and mother have been described in a widely quoted essay by the Rt. Rev. Kenneth E. Kirk, the late Bishop of Oxford. In his view, "The sex-relation once set up must have priority over all other natural relations." [18] The duties of wife and mother involve the "loving submission" [19] of wife to husband which would be threatened by the ordination of women priests, even if ordained women were celibate:

Even if ordination and matrimony were canonically declared to be mutually incompatible, so that no ordained women were allowed to marry, and no married women to be ordained, the wife and mother would be severely tempted to arrogate to herself a sexual equality with, if not superiority to, her husband analogous to the position of her ordained unmarried sister; dangerous strains would be introduced into domestic life; and the integrity of the Christian doctrine of the married relationship would be gravely challenged.[20]

The assumptions underlying this discussion of woman's role should be examined in the light of the Gospel message concerning the new life men and women share in Christ. In Chapter 5 we considered the view that women are subordinate to their husbands in their new life together in Christ. An examination of the biblical evidence concluded that there is no legitimate scriptural justification for the subordination of women to men in the Christian marriage relation or elsewhere in social life. The rule of men over their wives is clearly a result of the fall (Genesis 3:16) and is precisely one of those sinful conditions of human existence from which we have been saved by God's work for us in Christ.

The preeminent importance Bishop Kirk attaches to sexual and family relations in Christian life is problematic as well. This emphasis is not peculiar to those who oppose the ordination of women to the priesthood. It is frequently difficult—especially in America with its almost cultic emphasis on "togetherness" and family life—to untangle the Christian Gospel from visions of the "good life" projected by such secular sources as *Good Housekeeping* and the *Ladies' Home Journal.*

Bishop Kirk does have a scriptural basis for his assertion of the centrality of woman's role as wife and homemaker. He quotes from Genesis 1:28, in which God tells the first human couple, "Be fruitful and multiply, and fill the earth and subdue it." [21] (As this instruction is given to both Adam and Eve, one may wonder why fatherhood is not given more emphasis by Bishop Kirk.)

By contrast, we find that Jesus' teaching warns against preoccupation with family relations:

Do not think that I have come to bring peace on earth; I have not come to bring peace, but a sword. For I have come to set a man against his father, and a daughter against her mother, and a daughter-in-law against her mother-in-law; and a man's foes will be those of his own household. He who loves his father or mother more than me is not worthy of me; and he who loves his son or daughter more than me is not worthy of me; and he who does not take his cross and follow me is not worthy of me.
—Matthew 10:34–38

In his personal dealings with women, Jesus never gave special directions for their behavior as women; he treated them always as equals of men. In fact, if his attitude toward woman's role can be drawn from the Gospel reports, we would have to assert that he rejected a stereotyped view of woman as homemaker and childbearer. In Luke 10:41–42, the Lord gently rebukes Martha for her preoccupation with household duties; he would rather she acted as did Mary, who had chosen to listen to Jesus' teaching. On another occasion, he rejects the view that Mary his mother could be reduced to her reproductive functions. A woman in a crowd addresses Jesus saying, "Blessed is the womb that bore you and the breasts that you sucked!" To which Jesus replies, "Blessed rather are those who hear the word of God and keep it!" (Luke 11:27–28). According to Jesus, Mary's blessedness consisted not in maternity as such, but in her obedience to the will of God.[22]

Nor does Paul provide support for a Christian emphasis on family relations. In 1 Corinthians 7:7 he writes, "I wish that all were as I myself am. But each has his own special gift from God, one of one kind and one of another." Paul's own personal inclination was toward celibacy, but he was accepting of married life for those who chose it. Paul emphasizes the importance not of family life, but of the spiritual aspects of the new life we have in Christ, urging Christians to "earnestly desire the spiritual gifts" (1 Corinthians 14:1).

1 TIMOTHY 2:11–15

The author of 1 Timothy[23] strikes an unusual note in his insistence that "woman will be saved through bearing children" (2:15). The whole passage in which this phrase occurs has so frequently been used as a basis for defining the Christian woman's sphere that it should be considered carefully:

Let a woman learn in silence with all submissiveness. I permit no woman to teach or to have authority over men; she is to keep silent. For Adam was formed first, then Eve; and Adam was not deceived, but the woman was deceived and became a transgressor. Yet woman will be saved through bearing children, if she continues in faith and love and holiness, with modesty.— 1 Timothy 2:11–15

According to this New Testament writer, Eve is responsible for the fall and woman is therefore in a subordinate position to man even in our new life in Christ. In fact, Genesis divides the blame and the burdens of the fall between Adam and Eve (3:16–19), but this point has apparently eluded the writer. The author's emphasis on the subjugation of women falls short of conveying the Gospel message of forgiveness of sins and a new man-woman relationship "in Christ." What we are left with is the personal opinion of the writer that women are saved through childbirth.

This idea presents immediate difficulties because of its apparent inconsistency with other parts of the New Testament. 1 Timothy 2:15 is not easy to reconcile with Paul's injunctions to all Christians to desire spiritual gifts such as prophecy and with the conspicuous absence of motherhood from Paul's extended list of spiritual gifts in 1 Corinthians 12:27–28. As one commentator put it in a tongue-in-cheek aside, the notion of being saved through motherhood "does make salvation rather complicated for some of the Holy Virgins, but then, as Jesus remarked, 'With God all things are possible.' " [24]

Furthermore, the passage reflects a Jewish attitude toward motherhood which is no longer appropriate after the birth of the Messiah. André Dumas analyzes the Jewish attitude this way:

Before the birth of Christ woman was blessed as the mother of all living people. Her true and special priesthood was to bring into the world sons who would perpetuate the Chosen People until the coming of the Messiah. Her fruitfulness was a sign of the blessing of Yahweh.[25]

The coming of the Messiah changes woman's situation. She no longer has a "special priesthood" in her role as mother: "Since the birth of Christ maternity in itself is no longer a vocation which mediates grace." [26] Dumas points out that the "special priesthood" of women in childbearing was the fundamental reason for their exclusion from the priesthood of Israel.[27] To suggest that women may not be priests because they are all (potentially) mothers is "an anti-messianic regression": "Therefore one can no longer say: the ministry is for men, and maternity is for women. If one did, one would be failing to realise the radical difference between the Levitical priesthood and the Christic priesthood." [28]

THE CHRISTIC PRIESTHOOD

What is the nature of Christic priesthood? Perhaps we have a glimpse in Paul's second letter to the Corinthians:

Not that we are sufficient of ourselves to claim anything as coming from us; our sufficiency is from God, who has qualified us to be ministers of a new covenant, not in a written code but in the Spirit; for the written code kills, but the Spirit gives life. —2 Corinthians 3:5–6

Paul was a Jew and a freeman. But he does not claim that his ministry flowed from these things. The only thing sufficient for his ministry—and surely the only thing sufficient for the Christic priesthood—is "from God," the gift of the Holy Spirit.

CHAPTER
7

TIMES
AND
MEN'S
MANNERS

Opponents of the ordination of women to the priesthood
marshal a third type of theological argument—one that
carries much weight within Anglicanism. That argument is
that an all-male priesthood is a basic element in the faith
and tradition of Anglicanism which we are bound to maintain. The force of this argument derives from the fact that
Anglicans regard church tradition as an important source
of authority and guidance for Christian life today. Church
tradition is one of the elements of what a report of the
1968 Lambeth Conference of Anglican bishops termed
"our multiple inheritance of faith." [1] An outline of the elements of this inheritance provides a context in which to
discuss the claim that the ordination of women priests
would be a scandalous break with church tradition.

THE ANGLICAN INHERITANCE

According to the Lambeth Conference report mentioned
above, there are three strands to Anglican tradition. The
earliest strand includes, on the one hand, Scripture, and on

the other, "the Catholic Creeds set in their context of baptismal profession, patristic reasoning, and conciliar decision." A second strand of the Anglican tradition is found in the work of the sixteenth-century English reformation; for example, the Thirty-nine Articles of Religion and the Book of Common Prayer. The third strand embraces the "responsible witness to Christian truth" made within Anglicanism from the time of the English reformation. This aspect of the tradition includes scholarship, preaching, and the statements of Anglican Councils.[2]

What is the authority of this threefold tradition in the life of the church today? The Lambeth report answers this way:

To such a threefold inheritance of faith belongs a concept of authority which refuses to insulate itself against the testing of history and the free action of reason. It seeks to be a credible authority and is therefore concerned to secure satisfactory historical support and to have its credentials in a shape which corresponds to the requirements of reason.[3]

Anglicans do not accept tradition blindly, then, but in the light of reason. We welcome biblical and historical scholarship in our efforts to come to grips with the meaning of our faith-inheritance for the life of the church today; indeed, we consider such tools a part of our tradition. In this context we will examine the claim that church tradition rules out the ordination of women priests today.

THE VINCENTIAN CANON

The position of the opponents of women in the priesthood has been stated with clarity by E. L. Mascall:

The Anglican churches have never failed to pride themselves on their faithfulness to Scripture and primitive practice and to condemn those bodies which have innovated upon the Church's

faith and practice. It would be difficult to conceive a more
drastic innovation than the extension of Holy Orders to women;
for there can hardly be any aspect of the Church's practice
which conforms more closely to the Vincentian canon *Semper,
ubique et ab omnibus,* than the restriction of priesthood to the
male sex.[4]

The "Vincentian canon" to which the writer refers was a
principle set forth in the year 434 by Vincent, a monk of
Lérins, urging that "in the Catholic Church itself all possible care should be taken that we hold that faith which has
been believed everywhere [*ubique*], always [*semper*], and
by all [*et ab omnibus*]." [5]
The Vincentian canon is not, in fact, a piece of canon
law in the Episcopal Church, or even in the Roman Catholic Church. It serves instead as a theological guidepost for
discerning the fundamental tenets of our faith. The late
Bishop Kenneth E. Kirk (on other grounds an opponent of
the ordination of women to the priesthood) notes that there
are only "rare cases" in which the Vincentian canon can
be applied.[6] In those cases, he says, "nothing but absolute
and conscientious conviction after the most devout, exhaustive, and heartsearching inquiry would justify even
a momentary wavering of allegiance." [7] Catholic churches
have a long (and until lately, unbroken) tradition of an all-
male priesthood. Does the restriction of the priesthood to
males constitute one of those "rare cases" to which the
Vincentian canon may be applied?

A PECULIAR TRADITION

The Rev. Professor G. W. H. Lampe of Cambridge University has termed the all-male priesthood "tradition of a
peculiar kind." [8] It is a peculiar tradition in that it has both
wide acceptance and at the same time rests on an uncertain
foundation. For a long time, this tradition has been believed

to carry apostolic authority, putting it "among that class of
tradition by which the church is bound at all times." [9] This
belief, Lampe suggests, rests on the "mistaken assumption"
that the tradition was supported by "unchallengeable Scriptural authority" and "a general presupposition of the inferiority of women to men." [10]

Lampe's analysis is borne out when we look at the different strands of the Anglican tradition to see whether a doctrine of an all-male priesthood is part of that faith "believed
everywhere, always, and by all."

The most basic element in the faith-inheritance, Scripture, fails to provide support for a doctrine of an all-male
priesthood. In the preceding chapters we discussed in detail
the inadequacy of scriptural arguments against women in
the priesthood; it is necessary to emphasize only a few points
here. We should remember that the New Testament does
not offer any special arguments against women's participation in ministry. The limitations which the New Testament
imposes on woman's role in the church are always based on
her (assumed) subordinate role in creation or on her subordinate position after the fall. There is no "special" limita-
tion of woman's role in the church beyond the standard
limitations of propriety in the first-century Hellenistic world.
The theological basis (in Paul's interpretation of Genesis)
for these limitations cannot be maintained today. We are
called instead to implement the new relationship between
men and women that we have "in Christ."

Nor does one find in the creeds of the church an affirma-
tion of an all-male priesthood as one of the basic tenets of
the faith. To be sure, there are occasional pieces of canonical
legislation prohibiting women from Holy Orders[11] (hardly
surprising when one considers the opinions of some of the
church fathers concerning women),[12] but no evidence for
a doctrine of an all-male priesthood as a basic tenet of faith.
The Rev. Dr. J. Robert Wright of The General Theological
Seminary provides this historical summary:

The history of impediments against the reception of Holy Orders as seen in the early canons, in St. Thomas Aquinas, and even in impediments recognized by the Roman Catholic Church today, indicates that they have varied greatly and are all time-conditioned. *Examples:* In the early canons, one is disqualified from the office of priest if he has ever had a concubine; if he has married a widow, a divorced woman, a harlot, or an actress; or if he or his wife has ever committed adultery or fornication. When we look at St. Thomas Aquinas' understanding of the faith in the thirteenth century, we find that female sex is seen as an impediment to Holy Orders, for the reason "since it is not possible in the female state to signify eminence of degree, for a woman is in the state of subjection." (Note that he does not deny ordination to women by claiming that a priest is a symbol of a god who is masculine.) Aquinas would also deny ordination to those guilty of homicide, to those of servile status, and to those of illegitimate birth "since a man's good name is bedimmed by a sinful origin." [18]

INDELIBLE CHARACTER

Occasionally, an opponent of women in the priesthood will insist that St. Thomas was uttering more than a "time-conditioned" principle when he said that women were incapable of receiving the sacrament of Holy Orders. Women, it is suggested, cannot receive the "indelible character" of a deacon, priest, or bishop. But this argument, as Leonard Hodgson has shown, cannot be advanced without twisting the meaning of the terms "indelible" and "character" from their theological context and, at the same time, effectively denying that women may be members of the body of Christ.

The word "character," Hodgson points out, refers to "*spiritual* potency," not to physical attributes. In St. Thomas' terms, the priestly or episcopal character is given to the spirit, not the flesh. "So to say that a woman is incapable of receiving the priestly or episcopal character involves saying that her sexual differentiation carries with it a deficiency in spiritual receptivity and power." [14] Hodgson continues: "What then of 'indelible'? This simply means that in certain sacraments—baptism, confirmation, ordination—their grace is given once for all. They are not to be repeated." [15] If a woman cannot receive Holy Orders because of the "indelible character" of the sacrament, there is no reason to think that she can be validly baptized or confirmed, either.

THE ANGLICAN APPROACH

The fact is that the all-male priesthood is not part of the common mind of the church, found in Scripture and the Creeds and given deliberate theological formulation elsewhere. We are, therefore, under no solemn obligation to preserve it. Anglicans are deeply committed to the principle that traditions, even ancient ones, may be reconsidered and altered. Bishop Kirk describes the Anglican position thus:

In rejecting the claim of the papacy to an administrative supremacy *jure divino*, the Church of England once and for all committed herself to the position that no principle, however fully divine authority has been claimed for it in the past, is in fact exempt from reverent and unprejudiced reconsideration.[16]

The Anglican Articles of Religion provide explicit support for the view that customs which are time-conditioned may be reviewed and revised:

It is not necessary that Traditions and Ceremonies be in all places one, or utterly like; for at all times they have been divers, and may be changed according the diversity of countries, times, and men's manners, so that nothing be ordained against God's Word.[17]

When we draw on the threefold inheritance of faith, we do not find that tradition bars the ordination of women to the priesthood. An all-male priesthood is not an element

of the faith believed "everywhere, always, and by all." It is
one of those customs that may be changed as long as "nothing be ordained against God's Word." The vision of a new
man-woman relation "in Christ" leads us to reject the assumptions about the inferiority of women that have for so
long protected the tradition of an all-male priesthood from
critical reexamination. The report on "Women in the Priesthood" of the 1968 Lambeth Conference evaluated the
argument that our tradition prohibits women priests this
way:

If the ancient and medieval assumptions about the social role
and inferior status of women are no longer accepted, the appeal
to tradition is virtually reduced to the observation that there
happens to be no precedent for ordaining women to be priests.
The New Testament does not encourage Christians to think
that nothing should be done for the first time.[18]

CHAPTER
8

THE
PRACTICES
OF THE
CHURCHES
OF GOD

In his letter to the Corinthians, Paul concludes his argument that women should cover their heads in church by stating that "if anyone is disposed to be contentious, we recognize no other practice, nor do the churches of God" (1 Corinthians 11:16). In Paul's time, that was the end of the matter.

In our time, however, the churches of God recognize a great variety of practices concerning women, not only in the matter of their headgear, but in the matter of their ordination as well. We cannot simply say, "It's not done and that should be that," for in many of the churches of God women are eligible for every office along with men. Until recently, this could only be said of churches in the reform tradition, but in the past two decades churches that maintain the apostolic succession have begun ordaining women to the priesthood, too. Thus when we look to our sister churches, both Protestant and Catholic, for guidance on the question of women priests, we are given a wide range of suggestions and possible solutions. In this chapter we will explore the ecumenical dimensions of the question of women in the priesthood.

ANGLICANISM AS "THE BRIDGE CHURCH"

Anglicans tend to approach ecumenical dialogue with the attitude that, because our heritage is both Protestant and Catholic, we can fill a special role as mediator between the other churches. For the same reason, we tend to see ourselves as having a special relationship with the great Catholic churches that Protestant churches do not share. While our peculiar Anglican heritage should give us insight into the two worlds of Catholicism and Protestantism, we need to be cautious about overestimating our acceptability in either camp, and most especially in the Catholic. As one English theologian has remarked, bridges have more than one use.

"The bridge Church": that is a tempting metaphor, but only partly true. It is also a dangerously flattering metaphor. It gives us the comfortable assurance that we Anglicans are *the* people of God, indispensable to the divine strategy of reunion. But a bridge is a very static thing. It does not live; it cannot move. It neither goes forward nor backward. To stand permanently on a bridge is perilously like sitting on a fence.[1]

From our bridge vantage point, Anglicans have been slow to notice that churches, on both banks, have been redefining the role of women. These changes have been evident at every level of Protestant and Catholic church life, especially regarding the ordained ministry; and they have occurred not only in the United States, but throughout the world.

ORDINATION OF WOMEN ON THE
AMERICAN SCENE

The American church scene is probably the most diverse
national church situation in the world. We have in this
country over two hundred and thirty Christian denominations. We cannot survey the practices of all of them regarding the ordination of women, but it might be instructive
to look at a few of the major denominations.

A growing number of churches are ordaining women to
the full ministry on the same basis as men. The Southern
Baptist Convention, the largest American Protestant denomination, has recently begun ordaining women. The
American Baptist Convention ordains women as well. The
United Methodist Church has admitted women to full
ordination since 1956, as has the United Presbyterian
Church, U.S.A. The United Church of Christ has a long
history of full ordination for women, dating back to its
parent churches in the nineteenth century. In 1970 both
the Lutheran Church in America and the American Lutheran Church voted to extend full ordination to qualified
women. In June of 1972 Reform Judaism ordained its first
woman rabbi.[2]

In most of these denominations the last two years have
seen a renewed interest in the place of women in the church
at all levels. There are currently task forces on women and
the church at work on the national denominational level in
the United Methodist, United Presbyterian, United Church
of Christ, and the Lutheran Church in America. In every
case these task forces were initiated at the request of churchwomen who felt that women should have more voice at
every level of the church.

On the other hand, there are a number of major Christian bodies in the United States that do not fully ordain

women. The largest American church, the Roman Catholic Church, does not permit women within the sanctuary rail, much less ordain them. The Episcopal Church ordains women deacons but not priests. The Missouri Synod Lutheran Church does not ordain women, and none of the many Orthodox denominations ordain women.

Yet even in the denominations that do not ordain women fully there is a rising tide of self-assertion among the women, as seen in the informal grass-roots organizations of women pressing for a larger role in the Missouri Synod, the Episcopal Church, and the Roman Catholic Church. The American churches that do ordain women have, with a few exceptions especially among black churches, only begun to do so in the last two decades and in the case of the Lutheran churches in the last two years.[3]

ORDINATION OF WOMEN ON THE WORLD SCENE

In 1958, forty-eight member churches of the World Council of Churches (WCC) ordained women fully. The World Council of Churches reported in 1970 that seventy-two of its member churches had opened full ordination to qualified women. Since that time one Anglican and two Lutheran Synods have opened the priesthood to women, and it is likely that other member churches of the WCC have done so or will soon do so as well.

That events are moving faster than studies on this development can be seen by a brief look at the WCC's dealing with the question in the last ten years. The Third Assembly of the WCC, meeting in New Delhi in 1961, commissioned a study on the ordination of women. This study, *Concerning the Ordination of Women,* was submitted to a World Conference on Faith and Order which met in Montreal in 1963, and released in 1964. That group recom-

mended further study. At the fourth Assembly of the WCC
held at Uppsala, Sweden, in 1968, another consultation was
mandated to continue the study. That consultation was
held in Switzerland in September, 1970. However, between
1961 and 1970 more and more member churches of the
WCC independently made the decision to ordain women.

The 1964 document, *Concerning the Ordination of
Women,* is a scholarly and deliberate treatment of the subject. It is prefaced by cautionary words that this is not a
yes or no question and that "the basic attitude is . . . complicated, and many different points of view have to be considered, if one is to appreciate and understand the attitude
of the different churches." [4] The Report of the 1970 Consultation, however, urges change and experimentation. The
1970 Report, authored in part by the same theologian who
wrote the section of the 1964 Report quoted above, notes
this shift:

In the last few years the atmosphere has changed. A number
of new elements have entered the picture. The most important
are the following:

a) The number of churches which ordain women to the
ministry has considerably increased. . . .

b) The question has become an issue of serious discussion
in a larger number of traditions . . . this is particularly true
for the Roman Catholic Church. . . .

c) . . . In an increasing number of churches the burden of
proof is with those who are opposed to the ordination rather
than with those who affirm its appropriateness and necessity.

d) . . . it is more and more recognised that the ordination
does not necessarily threaten the cohesion of the ecumenical
fellowship. . . .[5]

Another new element in the 1970 Consultation was the
contribution of practicing ordained women and the first
reports of the actual experience of churches with women
ministers. Many of the members of the Consultation were
women ministers ready to share their experience. The Re-

port notes that "many churches ordain women who claim and give evidence of a call of the Holy Spirit. The ministry of these women is bearing fruit in the Church. . . ." [6] While some of the "pioneer" women ministers at the Consultation spoke of their loneliness and the hostility of some of their clerical colleagues, none regretted her decision to be ordained. Furthermore, it was noted that the "second generation" ministers seemed to have far fewer problems of this nature than the women who preceded them. In the words of a woman pastor of the Reformed Church of France:

Judging by the cases of two young women who have recently become pastors, who never knew the period prior to 1965 [the year that church began ordaining women] and who have thus started out on a path which has already been defined, I realise that they are certainly more at home in their ministry than we ourselves were just a few years ago, so I believe that as far as France is concerned the future for women seems very promising.[7]

A young woman priest from the Church of Sweden, pastor of a parish and chaplain in a prison, echoed the feeling that life was much easier for her and that she was much more readily accepted than the first women priests in that church just ten years ago.

Finally, the acceptance of women ministers varies within church families in different parts of the world. Thus Lutherans ordain women in most sections of Europe, but not in some areas of the United States. Reform churches have a wide variety of practice across the world, varying even from canton to canton in Switzerland. Anglicans have ordained women priests in Hong Kong but to date in no other Anglican church. Though ordination of women seems to be a matter of local option within church families, the 1970 Consultation also noted that the question seems most urgent in the United States and in the "third world" churches, the newly independent churches of Africa, Asia, and South America.[8]

Despite the pace of events on this question in the churches of the world in the past decade, there remain two large church families that do not ordain women to the priesthood anywhere in the world. These are of course the Roman Catholic and the Orthodox churches. Though at first glance they might seem isolated in their attitude toward women, we must remember that most of the world's Christians are either Orthodox or Roman Catholic.

The attitude of these two churches seems especially important to Anglicans, since we consider ourselves to be, with them, part of the Holy Catholic Church. The Anglican attitude toward other churches seems to vary, but for a number of Episcopalians, especially among the clergy, our relationship with the Catholic churches is of paramount importance. As one irate priest wrote to the author of an article on the ordination of women, "Don't you know that nobody cares *what* Protestants do?"

ROMAN CATHOLICS AND THE
ORDINATION OF WOMEN

The Rt. Rev. C. Kilmer Myers asserts that "the overwhelming majority of Christians cannot tolerate the idea of the ordination of women to the priesthood. For Anglicans to ordain them would produce a painful ecumenical tension." That the bishop is referring directly to the Roman Catholics can be seen by his next point, in which he warns us that "those Roman Catholics who speak in favor of the ordination of women to the priesthood do not represent the mainstream of their Church's tradition." The bishop seems unsure that this is so; however, he continues, ". . . the Roman Church is experiencing a crisis in identity which makes it difficult for *that* Church to be a guide for the rest of us." [9] Apparently the intolerance of the overwhelming majority of Christians is not as monolithic as he had earlier indicated.

Bishop Myers is not the only commentator who seems confused about the true dimensions of the issue of women priests on the ecumenical scene. When Anglican and Roman Catholic women began to meet and discuss the ordination of women several years ago, both groups were amazed to find that each had been told the most serious obstacle was ecumenical. The Anglican women had heard that Anglicans could not ordain women for fear of offending Rome. The Roman Catholic women had heard that Rome could not ordain women for fear of offending the Anglicans. As a result of this experience women in both churches are skeptical about the "ecumenical argument" against the ordination of women.

In both the Anglican and the Roman Catholic churches there have been great changes in the official position on the ordination of women in the past five years. Anglican changes date principally from the Lambeth Conference of 1968, but events in the Roman Catholic Church have been moving swiftly since the second session of the Second Vatican Council in 1963, when Cardinal Suenens of Belgium proposed that women be admitted as observers and was applauded by his brother bishops.[10]

Vatican II opened many doors in the Roman Catholic Church, and a new interest in the place of women in the church was one result of the deliberations. The Council made it possible for women to serve as lectors and, in some circumstances, to serve at mass. But events were adding to the impetus for change. In Latin America especially, nuns were assuming parochial duties due to a shortage of priests. In the aftermath of Vatican II a number of prominent Roman Catholic theologians ". . . publicly stated that they thought progress is possible on the question of the ordination of women." Among them were Bernard Haring, Jean Danielou, Georges Tavard, Gregory Baum, and Joseph Fichter.[11] But events were outstripping theological inquiry, and nuns in South America and altar girls in Holland were engaging in their own brand of aggiornamento.

That developments are still in progress in the Roman Catholic Church can be seen from recent questions raised about the ordination of women, not among the theologians, but among the bishops. The World Synod of Bishops meeting in Rome in October, 1971, was startled when the Canadian bishops "questioned the omission of ministries for women in the statement on priesthood." Cardinal Flahiff of Montreal proposed that the Synod ask the Pope to establish a mixed commission to study the question of women priests.[12]

Archbishop Leo C. Byrne of St. Paul-Minneapolis, chairman of a committee of American bishops on the role of women in church and society, recently received a statement endorsed by eight organizations of Catholic women calling for the ordination of women. Archbishop Byrne agreed in April, 1972, that his committee would make a full theological study of the issue.[13] As in Protestant churches, there are organized groups of women in the Roman Catholic Church who are insisting that the role of women in that institution be reexamined. Most notable among these is the St. Joan's Alliance, an international organization that has been working quietly since 1911 to improve the status of women.

Another development in the American Roman Catholic Church that promises some movement on the question of the ordination of women is the opening up of seminary education to women. At least two seminaries are currently admitting women students. We have seen in the experience of the American Episcopal Church that having women educationally qualified for priesthood moves the debate to an existential level.

Despite all these developments, however, it is still true that Roman Catholicism is a good deal further than Anglicanism from having women priests. The "ecumenical argument" mentioned above still has to recommend it the fact that Rome has no women priests at present. Also, unlike Anglicans, the Roman Catholics have canon laws that specifically limit priesthood to men. The question of how Roman Catholics view churches that do admit women to the priesthood still needs to be probed.

The first thing to be said is that since November, 1971, how Rome might react is no longer a theoretical question. The Anglican Church does have women priests, few and far away in Hong Kong to be sure, but in principle the line has been crossed. It has not come to our attention that the Roman Catholic Church is considering breaking off the scheduled talks on ministry as a result of the action of the Anglican Bishop of Hong Kong. Indeed, it would appear that the bishop is receiving more objections from within the Anglican Communion than from other churches.*

It has been our impression that Roman Catholics are watching developments within the Anglican Church on the question of women priests with interest rather than shock or dismay. Dr. Robert Wright, a member of the Anglican–Roman Catholic Consultation currently discussing ministry in the two churches, makes the same observation. He adds that "it seems unlikely that uniformity will be demanded on . . . canonical impediments to ordination. There will be agreement on fundamental theology, not on the parity of canon law." [14]

ROMAN CATHOLIC / PRESBYTERIAN / REFORM
DISCUSSIONS ON WOMEN

While Anglicans have been standing on the bridge, American Roman Catholics have been engaged in consultation

---

* For a full chronology of Hong Kong's nearly thirty-year struggle to ordain women priests, see Appendix A.

with members of the Presbyterian and Reformed churches on the subject of women in the church. The statement of this consultation, issued in October, 1971, is of interest, for it shows once more how open some Roman Catholics are on the question of the ordination of women to the priesthood.

The Consultation recommended to its parent bodies, "That qualified women be given full and equal participation in policy-making and decision-making, and voice in places of power, in the Churches on local, regional, national, and world levels." It further recommended: "(a) That seminary education in all the Churches be opened to qualified women; (b) that qualified women be admitted to ordination; (c) that in those Churches where the ordination of women presents theological difficulties and no theological study of the matter has been made, a theological committee be established immediately to investigate the problem and make recommendations." It also recommended that the parent bodies set up an ecumenical commission to implement the other recommendations and invite other denominations to join in the effort.[15]

That our continued movement toward priestly ordination for women might present difficulties with the Roman Catholic Church is a possibility. But we have no concrete evidence that this step would present a serious roadblock to reunion. The concluding statement of the Roman Catholic/Presbyterian/Reformed Consultation should give us hope that our Roman Catholic brothers and sisters will understand what we are doing. In discussing possible action for those churches that do not yet ordain women priests, the Consultation concludes:

The least that should be done is to test [the desire of women for ordination] . . . in accord with I Thess. 5:19, 21. The will of the Holy Spirit may be at stake here, as well as the personal rights of women members of these Churches. . . . To hesitate to take up the question in the most serious, competent and formal manner would suggest indifference to the will of the Holy Spirit, the personal rights of women, and the needs of the Church in its mission to the world.[16]

THE ORTHODOX POSITION
ON THE ORDINATION OF WOMEN

Nicolae Chitescu, an Orthodox theologian writing about the ordination of women for the 1964 WCC Report, begins his essay by setting forth the perspective from which his church approaches the question. He reminds us: "In the Orthodox Church the opinions of theologians do not count. The only thing that matters is the traditional regulations established by the Church as a whole in its canons and in its practice." [17]

If tradition is not to be changed, then there are many other issues besides the ordination of women on which our differences with Orthodoxy appear irreconcilable. Furthermore, if Dr. Chitescu's paper on the subject is any guide, we have already gone too far down the road of female ordination to be acceptable to Orthodoxy. Dr. Chitescu makes the point that though Orthodoxy had deaconesses until well into the twelfth century, they were not considered ordained, but merely had a "blessing" from the bishop to help him in his work.[18] Having admitted women to the diaconate on the same basis as men in a number of Anglican jurisdictions, we might expect that the Orthodox would have already stopped speaking to us. The fact that Anglicans are still in dialogue with them suggests that the ordination of women is not so serious an obstacle as had been imagined.

We have a great deal to learn from each other and a great deal to share, but our dialogues with the Orthodox must be carried on in an atmosphere of mutual respect. Just as we respect their conservation of their tradition, they must respect our reformulation of ours. As Dr. Robert Wright puts it, ". . . we must learn from them in many other matters, but their doctrinal method is just not one that is either western or Anglican." [19]

THE NATURE OF ECUMENISM

The Greek word from which "ecumenical" is derived means "the inhabited world." When we look at the current ecumenical movement in the churches in light of that root, we can extract several principles to keep in mind in our conversations with other Christians.

First, if we are to be truly ecumenical, we cannot choose those Christian bodies with which we feel more comfortable, and ignore the others. We cannot say that Protestants (or Catholics) don't count, for if Christians are to be reunited in their common faith in Christ no group that professes that faith can be ignored. Hence, if we are to be truly ecumenical we must talk and listen to those churches that do ordain women as well as to those who do not. Recent trends in ecumenical discussions are away from the idea of a "superchurch," an administratively reunited Christendom, and toward the idea of living together and alongside each other in spite of our differences. This approach does not gloss over the varying practices in the churches of God, but rejoices in the manifold ways in which God reveals himself to his people.

Secondly, if we are to be ecumenical we must first of all be true to ourselves, for our perception of the will of God for us is as valid as that of any other group of Christians. If we are called to follow the will of the Spirit as we hear it, we should not be concerned that other Christian groups are at different points in their understanding of that call. The ordination of women should be settled for us by what we feel the Holy Spirit calls *us* to do, not by what some other group might think about it. Anglicans watch with interest the debate over clerical celibacy in the Roman Catholic Church, but we view it as that church's problem despite whatever ecumenical ramifications it might have for us. We do not suggest to the Roman Catholics that if they want to continue to talk to Anglicans they had better allow their clergy to marry. For the same reason they do not suggest that we not ordain women priests.

Finally, we should see ecumenism as going somewhere. We should keep in mind that the object of all this talk is to make it possible for Christians to work together in implementing God's plan for the world. When we allow ourselves to become sidetracked on whether or not we can live with each other's practices, whatever those might be, we are in danger of losing sight of the ecumenical goal.

CHAPTER
9

"YES,
BUT . . . "

In the preceding chapters we have tried to deal with what we consider to be the basic issues in the debate about women in the priesthood. In the first few chapters we tried to clear the ground of the usually unexpressed but very real doubts people may feel about women priests, and to look at some of the possible roots of those doubts in their feelings about priesthood and their feelings about women. In the next three chapters we considered theological arguments and their basis in Scripture and church tradition. In the chapter preceding this one we looked at the ramifications the priestly ordination of women might have ecumenically.

In addition to these issues, other arguments are sometimes offered against the ordination of women. These objections are often offered as "yes, but" considerations. However biblically and theologically sound the ordination of women may be, opponents ask if we have really thought about these minor-but-important considerations which rule out women priests in this church at this time. In this chapter we will examine some of the most common "yes, but" objections to women priests.

THE OVERSUPPLY OF CLERGY

In the past few years Episcopalians have been made painfully aware that there are too many priests for the existing church-related and funded jobs available. A quick check of the 1960 and 1971 editions of the *Church Annual* shows that in 1970, there were 68 fewer parishes and 3,183 more clergy than there were in 1959.[1] Any bishop or ordinand can vouch for the fact that the job market in the Episcopal Church is tight and likely to become more so in the face of a continued uncertain economic picture for society as a whole. Why, then, we are asked, do we suggest adding to this problem by admitting a whole new class of people, namely women, to an already overcrowded profession?

The hidden assumption in this "economic argument" seems to be that admitting women to priesthood will automatically swell the total number of priests, perhaps even double it. This possibility is highly unlikely. The report of a 1966 study committee of the House of Bishops was no doubt correct in its assertion that it is ". . . unlikely that any great number of women would seek ordination . . . and at the least there need be no fear that women will 'take over' the Church." [2]

It is understandable that clergy are apprehensive about adding women to an already uncertain job market and thereby adding yet another variable and even more competition for the few jobs there are. But for the forseeable future the number of women who will be called to priesthood and the variety of ministries in which they will engage should make them a very minor economic threat.

The Rt. Rev. Stephen F. Bayne, Dean of The General Theological Seminary, has objected to the term "oversupply of clergy" on the ground that the suggestion that there are too many priests calls into question the workings of the Holy Spirit in priestly ordinations, and that it "verges on impiety and disobedience to speak of the church having too many priests." He suggests instead that "the problem is not one of too many priests—it is one of too few imaginative and effective ways in which priests and priesthood are being put to work in the church." [3] That the institutional church

is failing to deploy its clergy effectively is clear, but that is
no reason to declare a moratorium on ordination.

"THERE ARE ASPECTS OF PRIESTHOOD WOMEN CAN'T HANDLE."

Another "yes, but" argument we often hear is that there are
some aspects of priesthood that women simply could not
manage. Examples are usually along the line of midnight
calls to dangerous neighborhoods or counseling men with
embarrassing sexual problems. Yet these are not situations
peculiar to priesthood, though they might be aspects of
priesthood in a particular setting. These are the sort of
problems that women doctors and social workers also run
into and they have not proved insurmountable to women
in those fields. In fact, laywomen have encountered similar
occurrences in parish work and have managed to cope with
them.

Another area in which difficulties are said to arise for a
woman priest is that of hearing confession. It might be that
a person would be unable to confess some things to a woman
priest and this does perhaps present difficulties for some
people. Yet at present there are woman communicants who
are in the predicament of being unable or unwilling to
confess to male priests and who are simply going without
confession (and absolution) as a result. Our experience
tells us that some people, both women and men, would
find it possible, even preferable, to confess to a woman. It
is reasonable to assume that most men could relate to a
female priest just as most women can relate to a male priest.
However, there are occasions when one wants to talk specifically with a member of his own or the opposite sex. For
this reason it would be desirable to have confessors of both
sexes available.

"WHEN WOMEN ENTER A PROFESSION, MEN LEAVE IT."

Some people argue that for the good of the Episcopal Church we should not ordain women. They reason that the church is already a female-dominated institution.* We should not drive out the few remaining men by allowing women to "take over." They suggest that all the decision-making jobs in the church should be reserved for men. From their point of view the only way to keep the men coming to church is to make them feel important.

This argument seems to us insulting to the integrity of the men of the church. If the only reason men attend church is that they can feel powerful as clergy or vestrymen, we haven't done a very good job of preaching the Gospel within the church itself. We do not believe that many churchmen's commitment is proportionate to the authority they hold in church, nor that they are so immature as to need to be made to feel important. Perhaps without realizing it some men have come to count on feeling important at church and would be hurt if asked to share leadership with women. But Christian women do no favor for Christian men when they try to "protect" men's position in the church by limiting that of women.

"WE CAN'T IMAGINE A WOMAN RECTOR."

Though the objection to women rectors is often initially supported by the contention that women do not make good administrators or that they lack the authority to hold a parish together, illustrations of women administrators in other fields fail to lay it to rest. The reason is that the real objection is aesthetic—we simply cannot imagine Sunday services being led by a woman. We feel that the liturgy de-

* This is borne out by the fact that most American Protestant churches have found that their membership is close to 60 percent female.

mands a bass, or at least a baritone voice to do it justice.
Women's voices do not ring with the authority and power
we find so comforting in the familiar liturgy.

We fail to take into account two factors when we rest our
case on this objection. The first is that we have so little
experience with women trained to read well that we are not
in a position to make a fair judgment on the relative beauty
of male- and female-led services. We are also, being human,
very apt to prefer what we are used to and to view it as
aesthetically superior to anything innovative.

Even if we decide we are certain we could not endure a
female rector, we must remind ourselves that all priests are
not rectors and that there are a number of effective male
priests we wouldn't want as rectors either. There are male
priests who stutter or who have reading difficulties, and
many of these men exercise effective priestly ministries in
areas other than public worship. So often when discussing
women in priesthood we leap to the image of woman rector
in a large, cavernous church with bad acoustics. Though
some women could fill this role as admirably as could some
men, prohibiting all women from answering a call to priesthood because some might be unsuited for some aspects of
particular calls doesn't make much sense.

ORDINATION OF WOMEN AND "THE ESTABLISHMENT"

Much of the recent writing against the ordination of women
to the priesthood hints very broadly that the issue is not
ordination, but whether rank and file Episcopalians will
allow "the establishment" to perpetrate upon them a
change of which they do not approve. Similar changes cited
in the church's recent past are the funding of General Convention Special Program and the new trial liturgies of the
Green Book. These changes are said to be abhorrent to most

Episcopalians, and allegedly have come about due to the current attempt to run the church "... according to the will of the Presiding Bishop and his tight little party of followers. They are past masters in the art of lobbying and forcing their will on the majority." [4]

When people speak of an "establishment" or a small group bent on a certain end it is best to stop and ask whom they mean. GCSP and the Green Book were both approved by General Conventions of the Episcopal Church, an establishment that includes nearly eight hundred representatives of dioceses and missionary districts. The Executive Council of the church might be considered an establishment, but to the best of our knowledge that group has never discussed women in the priesthood. The staff of Executive Council may hold a variety of opinions on this matter, but they are far too busy just keeping the machinery running to be engaging in conspiracies. To deal in innuendoes does not further the debate on women in the priesthood.

"THE WOMEN OF THE CHURCH DON'T WANT WOMEN PRIESTS."

That there are women who disapprove of the ordination of women to the priesthood we have no doubt. We have in fact spoken with some of these women and discussed the matter with them, sometimes changing their views, sometimes not. What we are not at all certain of, however, is that *most* churchwomen are opposed. In fact, the only official count of women's opinion we have any record of is the vote of the 1970 Triennial Meeting of the Women of the Church. These women, representing the organized women of the dioceses and missionary districts, voted by a nearly five to one margin in favor of a resolution to support the ordination of women to the diaconate, priesthood, and episcopate. It was the patient persistence of many of

these same women that finally resulted in the Houston
Convention's opening the diaconate to women on the same
basis as men.

It is interesting to note that most often it is clergymen
who tell us that women are opposed. Often they can cite
numerous women in their parishes who have expressed dis-
approval. Yet as Margaret Ermarth, a Lutheran authority
on this subject, has observed, when the issue is women in
the priesthood, in almost every church it has been the
clergy who have objected most strenuously.[5] Our church
is no exception, for it was by a narrow margin in the clergy
order of the House of Deputies that the resolution to ordain
women priests was defeated in 1970. This should come as
no surprise, for it is the clergy that would be most directly
affected by this change. When the question was seating
women as lay delegates, it was the lay order in the House
of Deputies that consistently voted it down.

"WOMEN PRIESTS WILL MEAN SCHISM IN THE CHURCH."

One of the reasons some opponents cite for continuing not
to ordain women to the priesthood is that such a move will
"split the church." A number of clergy have clearly stated
that they intend to leave the Episcopal Church if we
ordain woman priests. There is also a move afoot to break
off communion with the Diocese of Hong Kong because
there are women priests functioning there.

It seems strange that the church should fear the loss of a
number of priests, yet seems to have no qualms about the
number of theologically educated women we have lost as
clergy to other denominations because of our inability to
use their talents.[6] We have also lost the talents of many
laywomen and some men because they could not stay in a
church that refused to recognize women as equal partners
with men.

"WOMEN IN THE PRIESTHOOD WOULD DOWNGRADE THE ROLE OF MARY."

People who advocate the ordination of women to the priesthood are sometimes accused of being contemptuous of the special place of the Virgin Mary in Christian tradition. Women, we are told, should find more than enough to keep them busy in emulating our Lord's mother. She was not an apostle or even a deaconess.

We do not intend to downgrade the position of Mary in tradition or Scripture. What we find in Scripture is a young woman who said yes to God's call despite the certain shame and disgrace this answer would bring to her family as well as herself. We rejoice with her in the powerful and courageous words of her song of rejoicing—the Magnificat. In the words of the Roman Catholic theologian Hans Küng, she is "the first among believers" and we venerate her for her courage and faithfulness to the will of God.

This is the only way we know how to venerate her—it is manifestly impossible for any modern woman to emulate her state of virgin-motherhood or to see herself as "Theotokos," God-bearer, for that role is Mary's alone. The only way we can honor her is by attempting to appropriate her courage and faithfulness to the will of God. Many women feel that is exactly what they are doing in their effort to respond to God's call to them to become priests.

THE FORCE OF "YES, BUT" ARGUMENTS

We have looked at some of the more common "yes, but" arguments against women in the priesthood in some detail. There are others, some silly, some obscure, some mystical, but all offered in the sincere belief that for this reason alone women should not be priests and that should be an end to it.

While we do not question the sincerity of those who offer arguments of this nature as final and compelling, we would ask them to give their opposition to the priesthood for women more serious thought. Are they really opposed because jobs are scarce or because clergy would leave or because they think a woman celebrant would prove "distracting" to male communicants? Or is their opposition rooted elsewhere, perhaps in the way they feel about women or the church or the Gospel message? Perhaps with C. S. Lewis they feel that when we mix women and religion we are dealing with "the live and awful shadows of realities utterly beyond our control."

Christ has freed us by his death and resurrection from the "powers and principalities," the evil forces beyond our control which, wholly without our permission, clamor to govern our lives. Jesus himself was impatient with people who said "yes, but" as in the parable of the banquet (Luke 14:16–24), where no excuse for not attending the feast is acceptable to the host. Christians are free to direct their own lives, but they are also obligated to try to understand their own feelings and judge them in the light of Christ's freeing work.

EPILOGUE:

DO NOT QUENCH THE SPIRIT*

The fundamental issue in all the deliberations about the ordination of women to the priesthood is the willingness of the church to test the work of the Holy Spirit. There are Episcopal women who claim to be called to the office and ministry of priesthood. If they were men, the church would permit that call to be tested through the processes set up in the canons of the church. To forbid women the opportunity to test their vocations in the same way comes perilously close to denying the possibility of the work of the Holy Spirit in the lives of these women.

An English bishop remarked after meeting Dr. Margit Sahlin, one of the first women priests in the Church of Sweden, "If anyone asks me in future whether I believe in women priests I can only say that I have seen one. And by any tests known to the Gospel, I find myself unable to deny the grace of orders or to resist the Holy Spirit." [1]

There is only one way to learn whether the ordination of women to the priesthood is "of God" and that one way is to try it. The efficacy of a man's ministry is tested by the fruits of the Spirit that result. The only way to test the priesthood of women is to allow women with vocations to follow their call.

* 1 Thessalonians 5:19.

Appendix A

CHRONOLOGY OF MAJOR ANGLICAN DOCUMENTS and Actions Concerning Women in Holy Orders, 1862–1972

(Documents and actions of the Episcopal Church in the United States are designated with an asterisk.)

1862   Ancient order of deaconesses restored in Anglicanism when Bishop of London orders a deaconess with the laying on of hands.

*1885, Bishops of Alabama and New York order deaconesses
*1887   with the laying on of hands.

*1889 General Convention authorizes the "setting apart" of deaconesses by canon.

1919   *The Ministry of Women,* report of a commission appointed by the Archbishop of Canterbury to reconsider the office of deaconess, published in England.

1920   Lambeth Conference (the regular meeting of all Anglican bishops held every ten years) resolves that "ordination of a deaconess confers on her holy orders."

1930   Lambeth Conference withdraws the assertion that deaconesses are in Holy Orders.

1935   Report of a commission on the ministry of women appointed by Canterbury and York, published in England. Finds no compelling theological reasons for or against the ordination of women, but affirms the male priesthood "for the Church to-day."

1944   Bishop R. O. Hall of Hong Kong ordains the Rev. Li Tim Oi to the priesthood. Canterbury and York repudiate the ordination and the Rev. Li Tim Oi resigns her orders.

1948   Lambeth Conference denies Hong Kong's request for permission to order women as priests on an experimental basis, on the grounds that "the time has not come" to consider the matter. Lambeth urges renewed emphasis on the role and work of deaconesses.

*1964   General Convention (St. Louis) changes the wording in the canon on deaconesses to read "ordered" rather than "appointed" and to allow the marriage of deaconesses.

*1965   Acting on the basis of the 1964 canon change, the Rt. Rev. James Pike, Bishop of California, recognizes Deaconess Phyliss Edwards as a deacon by virtue of her prior ordination as a deaconess. In a ceremony in San Francisco, he confers on her the New Testament and stole, historic marks of the diaconate.

*1966   House of Bishops receives preliminary report it commissioned in 1965 on "The Proper Place of Women in the Ministry of the Church." The House of Bishops recommends that the Lambeth Conference of 1968 study the question of the ordination of women to the priesthood.

1968   Lambeth Conference refers question of the ordination of women to the priesthood back to the provinces of world Anglicanism for further study. Lambeth endorses principle that deaconesses are within the diaconate. Anglican churches (*e.g.*, Hong Kong, Kenya, Korea, Canada) begin ordaining women to the diaconate.

*1969   Special General Convention (South Bend) changes canon so that women may be licensed to be lay readers and to administer the chalice.

*1970   Joint Commission on Ordained and Licensed Ministries reports to General Convention (Houston) and recommends that all orders of ministry—diaconate, priesthood, episcopacy—be opened to women immediately. Report rejected by narrow margin in the clergy order in the House of Deputies.

*1970   Triennial Meeting of Episcopal Church Women (Houston) considers the report of the Joint Commission on Ordained and Licensed Ministries and votes to endorse the report by a margin of 222–45.

*1970   General Convention (Houston) declares deaconesses to be within the diaconate. Convention changes canon on deaconesses to permit women to be ordained deacons under the same regulations as men.

1971   Anglican Consultative Council (world Anglican body of clergy and laity meeting between Lambeth Conferences) declares that it "will be acceptable" if a bishop ordains women priests with the approval of his Province (or Synod, in the case of Hong Kong).

1971   The Rt. Rev. Gilbert Baker, Bishop of Hong Kong, with the approval of his Synod and having been told by the Council of Southeast Asia that the Council had no jurisdiction in the matter, ordains two women deacons, the Rev. Jane Hwang and the Rev. Joyce Bennett, to the priesthood.

*1971   The House of Bishops, having put the question of the ordination of women on the agenda of its meeting, refers the matter to a committee of bishops for further study.

*1972   Various dioceses prepare resolutions for the 1973 General Convention, urging the ordination of women to the priesthood. Other dioceses resolve to study the question.

Appendix B

REPORT OF THE JOINT COMMISSION
on Ordained and Licensed Ministries, 1970

The Joint Commission on Ordained and Licensed Ministries was established by Special Convention II, and its members were appointed by the Presiding Bishop and the President of the House of Deputies. Pursuant to the Joint Rules of the two Houses, the Commission makes this report to the Sixty-Third General Convention.

The Commission has met in compliance with the direction of the resolution creating it, "to study the question of the ordination of women and the licensing of women as Lay Readers, giving special attention to the advisability of amending Article VIII of the Constitution and Canons 34, 49 and 50." Such study has resulted in the entire Commission unanimously reaching the following conclusions:

1. All members of the Body of Christ, both male and female, are called to the work of the ministry. The Holy Spirit gives all members of that Body the power to share with Christ the mission for God and for the world, regardless of their sex.

2. The inferior social role and status given women in other cultures may have been a valid reason for denying them the

special ministry of the ordered priesthood and the ordained and consecrated episcopate. In the culture where the Episcopal Church is now at work, however, the equality of the social role and status of men and women is a valid reason for insisting that women no longer be denied any ministry, general or special, which is empowered by the Spirit of God alone.

3. Every moment that the Church continues categorically to deny either the ordered priesthood or the consecrated episcopate to a person competent to hold those offices in our culture today, because she is a woman, it does far more than exclude one woman from a specific ministry or a specific apostolate. Such a denial is also a continuous signal from the Church that all persons in the category of woman are intrinsically inferior creatures who should also serve only as auxiliaries to men in the general ministry and the general apostolate of all believers. Untold numbers of women within and without the Church are receiving the Church's signals "loud and clear"!

4. The language of the Constitution, Canons and Ordinal of the Prayer Book permits the opening of the priesthood and the episcopacy to women by the interpretive action of a single Convention. The urgent needs of the Church and the World impel the conclusion that the short route of interpretation should be taken rather than the long, tortuous, uncertain and unnecessary route of amending the Constitution, Canons and Prayer Book.

5. Opening the priesthood and episcopacy to women would be consonant with the actions taken by the House of Bishops in its 1966 Meeting in response to the Report of its Committee to Study the Proper Place of Women in the Ministry of the Church. It would also be consonant with the Report of the 1968 Lambeth Conference Committee on "Women and Priesthood," and it would not violate any restrictions placed on any part of the Anglican Communion by the Resolutions of the Conference itself. Such action would be responsive to the recent memorials and petitions to this Con-

vention, including memorials from the Dioceses of Central New York, Maryland and Ohio.

6. Canon 49 generally disqualified women as licensed Lay Readers by restricting the office to "a competent male person." The disqualification has already been removed by Special Convention II. That Convention opened the office to women by: (a) amending the Canon through deletion of the word "male"; (b) interpreting the referent pronouns "he," "him" and "his" to be generic words which included females as well as males.

In the light of these conclusions, supported by the subsequent portions of this Report, the Commission recommends adoption of the following resolution by the 63rd General Convention:

RESOLUTION

WHEREAS, the General Convention of the Episcopal Church has interpreted generic words to include both males and females; and

WHEREAS, the interpretative authority of General Convention extends to include the words "Bishop," "Priest" and "Deacon," together with the referent pronouns "he," "his" and "him" where these words appear in Articles II, III and VIII of the Constitution, the Canons pertinent to ordination, and the Ordinal of the Book of Common Prayer; therefore, be it

RESOLVED, the House of _____ concurring, That the Sixty-Third General Convention of the Church affirms that women have equal rights with men in the Episcopal Church, including the right to seek and accept ordering to the diaconate and to the priesthood and ordination and consecration to the episcopate; and it further affirms the right of the Church to ordain and consecrate women as well as men; and be it further

RESOLVED, the House of _____ concurring, That the General Convention hereby interprets the words "Bishop," "Priest" and "Deacon" together with the referent pronouns "he," "his" and "him," and other related words, wherever these words appear in the Constitution, Canons, Ordinal of the Book of Common Prayer and other official documents with regard to ordination and consecration, to include both males and females.

Joint Commission on Ordained and Licensed Ministries:
The Rt. Rev. Dean T. Stevenson, S.T.D., Chairman
The Rev. Henry H. Rightor, D.D., Virginia Theological Seminary, Secretary
The Rt. Rev. David K. Leighton, D.D.
Miss Pauli Murray, J.S.D., Massachusetts
Mr. William M. Passano, Maryland
Deaconess Frances Zielinski, Central House for Deaconesses, Illinois

ANNEX A: HISTORY OF THE MOVEMENT TO OPEN
THE PRIESTHOOD AND EPISCOPATE TO WOMEN

The idea of opening the priesthood to women is no outrageously new concept or fad. In March of 1916 William Temple wrote: "Personally I want (as at present advised) to see women ordained to the priesthood." Temple's biographer, F. A. Iremonger, commented, "He championed the cause of women, not because they were women but because they were human beings whose personality was sacred in the sight of God . . ." [*William Temple, Archbishop of Canterbury* (London and New York: Oxford Press, 1948), p. 305].

Since the time of William Temple's statement, thinking and writing on the subject of women and the ordained ministry has continued in the fields of missions, biblical studies, theology, doctrine, sociology, etc. Instead of attempting to plough the same ground again, an appropriate portion of the comprehensive Report of the House of Bishop's Committee to Study the Proper Place of Women in the Ministry of the Church (1966) is attached as Appendix 1 to this report.

PROGRESS REPORT TO THE HOUSE OF BISHOPS
from
THE COMMITTEE TO STUDY THE PROPER PLACE OF WOMEN
IN THE MINISTRY OF THE CHURCH

October, 1966

The creation of the Committee to Study the Proper Place of Women in the Ministry of the Church was authorized by the House of Bishops in September, 1965, and its members were subsequently appointed by the Presiding Bishop. The Committee consists of: The Bishop of Rochester, Chairman; Mrs. Irvin Bussing of California, Secretary; The Bishop of New Hampshire; The Bishop of Oklahoma; Mrs. Charles M. Hawes III of the Virgin Islands; Rev. Dr. Alden D. Kelley of Bexley Hall; Mrs. Theodore O. Wedel of New York.

Of the women serving on the Committee, one has been an executive in public relations and advertising, another has been engaged in professional Church work for many years, both in this Church and on an ecumenical level, and the third has recently received a Bachelor of Divinity degree.

The Committee presents this preliminary Report, indicating the direction of its thinking and making some initial recommendations to the House of Bishops.

Scope and Urgency

The Committee presents this preliminary Report, indicating the place of women in the Church's ministry demands the facing of the question of whether or not women should be considered eligible for ordination to any and all Orders of that Ministry. No one would deny that women are part of the lay ministry of the Church, and the Committee does not think that another examination of the status of Deaconesses alone would do justice to the matter.

The Committee is convinced that a number of factors give the question a new urgency, require a fresh and unprejudiced look at the whole issue, and warn against uncritical acceptance of beliefs, attitudes, and assumptions that have been inherited from the past and strongly persist at the present time. Three such factors seem especially important:

a. *The growing place of women in professional, business, and public life,* in medicine, in teaching, in politics and government, in the Armed Forces, even in high executive positions within this Church.

b. *The development of new forms of ministry* that permit greater flexibility and call for many more specialized skills than is the case when the ministry is limited largely to one priest in charge of one parish, a generalist rather than a specialist. As one member of the Committee put it, "We need to stop talking or thinking of the ministry as though it were a single unitary vocation. Rather, we need to think of the many functions of ministry which are needed today—the sacramental ministry, preaching, theological and Biblical research, teaching, pastoral work and counseling, social service, etc. In an age of specialization and of a tremendous explosion of knowledge we must face the fact that no one person can possibly be adequate in all these areas. . . . We need to encourage specialization according to a person's gifts and interests and organize our corporate life to use specialists." This fact requires consideration of how women may be used in a changing and increasingly specialized ministry.

c. *The growing importance of the issue in ecumenical relationships.* The question is being discussed in many parts of the Anglican Communion. . . . The initiation of a study of the experiences of ordained women was urged by the World Conference on Church and Society, meeting at Geneva in the summer of 1966. In this country, the Consultation on Church Union has reached the point of considering the drafting of a plan of union, involving this Church and a number of others that now admit women to the ordained ministry, and the question of the ordination of women in such a united Church obviously must be faced as the negotiations proceed.

Nor does it seem that the question of the ordination of women in the Orthodox and Roman Churches can be regarded as finally and forever decided in the negative, particularly in view of other changes that have occurred, especially in the Roman Church.

There is a sentence in one of the official documents of Vatican II that reads, "Since in our times women have an ever more active share in the whole life of society, it is very important that they participate more widely also in the various fields of the Church's apostolate" [*The Documents of Vatican II*, Walter M. Abbott, S.J., General Editor, (New York: Guild Press, 1966), p. 500.] The Archbishop of Durban, South Africa, Dr. Dennis Hurley, recently predicted that "there are going to be some fantastic developments in the role of women in the Church." (See *Christian Century*, September 15, 1966.) And in an interview with the Secretary of this Committee, given on October 11, 1966, the Rev. Dr. Hans Küng, Professor in the University of Tubingen (Germany) stated, "There are two factors to consider regarding the ordination of women to the Sacred Ministry of the Church. The first is that there are no dogmatic or biblical reasons against it. The second is that there are psychological and sociological factors to be considered. The solution to the problem depends on the sociological conditions of the time and place. It is entirely a matter of cultural circumstances."

Burden of Proof

The Committee has become increasingly convinced that the burden of proof is on the negative in this matter.

For, to oppose the ordination of women is either to hold that the whole trend of modern culture is wrong in its attitude toward the place of women in society, or to maintain that the unique character of the ordained ministry makes that ministry a special case and justifies the exclusion of women from it.

Reasons Given Against the Ordination of Women

Mental and Emotional: The alleged mental and emotional characteristics of women are said to make them unsuitable to serve as clergymen. Such arguments are never very clear, consistent, or precise. Sometimes, the weakness of women is stressed, despite the fact that women are healthier and live longer than men. Or, it is claimed that women think emotionally rather than rationally and that they over-personalize problems or decisions.

The same sort of arguments could be used to show that women are unfit for almost any business, professional, or public responsibility. They were used against the admission of women to higher education, to the practice of medicine and law, and against women suffrage. They are still being used against the admission of women to the House of Deputies of the General Convention.

None of these negative arguments has been borne out in any other walk of life. Women have proved to be capable, often brilliant, lawyers, statesmen, scientists, and teachers. They have enriched the practice of medicine, and politics have neither been redeemed nor debased by their participation.

As experience has demonstrated, only experience can show the extent to which women might fulfill a useful role in the ordained ministry, as well as ways in which their role might be different from the role of men. Here, as in other callings, women would need to be better than men in order to compete with them.

Emil Brunner states, "It is absolutely impossible to put down in black and white, as a universal rule, which spheres of activity 'belong' to women and which do not. This can only become clear through experience; and for this experience, first of all the field must be thrown open."

Because the field has not been thrown open, any judgment based on the Church's experience with professional women workers is limited and inadequate. With the highest respect for the contributions these women are now making, the Committee is convinced that an absolute bar at the level of ordination has a deterring effect upon the number of women of high quality who enter professional Church work or undertake theological study, and that the same bar places theologically trained women in a highly uncomfortable and anomalous position.

Marriage Versus Ministry: There is alleged the impossibility or impracticality of combining the vocation of a clergyman with domestic responsibilities, with marriage, as well as the bearing and care of children. Would it be possible for a wife and mother of a family to bring to the priesthood the required degree of commitment, concentration, and availability?

First, it must be said that many women choose careers and never marry, others combine marriage and careers. The Church recognizes that the latter is an entirely legitimate vocation, both in the secular world and in the Church itself.

Secondly, the question of married women is partly answered by the fact that married men are permitted to serve as bishops, priests and deacons in the Anglican Communion. Such permission implies an acknowledgment of the strong claims that the wife and family of a married clergyman rightfully have upon his time, his money, and the conduct of his vocation. All would grant that a clergyman has a duty, as well as a right, to take into account his wife's health, or his children's education, in considering a call, in negotiating about his salary, in determining his standard of living and the amount of money he will give away.

While other, and perhaps more serious, problems might exist for a woman who wished to combine ordination with marriage, the Commission is by no means convinced that such a combination would not prove practical in many instances. Even such demanding professions as teaching and medicine are finding ways of using skilled and trained married women with children, both on a part-time and a full-time basis. Many intelligent women find that they are better wives and mothers by combining an outside calling with the care of a family. Many also can look forward to years of full-time professional work after their children are grown.

The Commission would ask whether the leadership of the Church does not possess resourcefulness and imagination similar to that displayed by other institutions in using married women, if not often as ministers in charge of parishes, yet as assistants, or for the specialized types of ministry that are sure to develop much more rapidly in the future. It is thought unlikely that any great number of women would seek ordination, considering the very real difficulties involved. But difficulty is not impossibility, and at the least there need be no fear that women will "take over" the Church.

Theological Arguments: Then there are certain theological objections which seem to the Committee to present a strange mixture of tradition and superstition.

Biblical: Some of the objections rest on a rather literal approach to the Bible and fail to take into account the degree to which the Bible is conditioned by the circumstances of its time. It is not necessary to dwell upon the Creation Story, in which woman is created after man and taken from him, nor be influenced by the fact that women were excluded from the covenant-relation of God with Israel, any more than one would support polygamy or slavery because both have clear sanction in the Old Testament. Nor is one moved by the familiar argument that our Lord chose only men to be his apostles. Any sound doctrine of the Incarnation must take full account of the extent to which Jesus lived and thought within the circumstances and environment of his own time. To deny such facts is to deny the full humanity of Jesus and to subscribe to a grotesque Docetism. Our Lord did choose women as close associates, even if he did choose men as the transitional leaders of the new Israel. The Committee also believes that St. Paul, as well as the authors of Ephesians and the Pastoral Epistles, were sharing in the passing assumptions of their own time, as well as advising wise strategy for the First Century Church, in recommending that women keep silent at services, cover their heads, and be subordinate to their husbands; just as St. Paul thought it wise to send a run-away slave back to his master. Much more permanent and basic are St. Paul's words, "There is neither Jew nor Greek . . . slave nor free . . . male nor female; for you all are one in Christ Jesus."

Image of God: Then, there is a cluster of theological objections based on the assumption that the female is a less true or complete image of God than the male; and that, therefore, woman is less capable, or is quite incapable, of representing

God to man and man to God in the priesthood, and of receiving the indelible grace of Holy Orders.

This line of reasoning has a number of curious sources. In the Bible, God is thought and spoken of as "he," for the most part, as would be entirely natural in a culture first militant and warlike, always patriarchal, and with a developing monotheism. Even so, God can be compared with a mother who comforts her child.

Jesus Christ was born a man. Obviously, God's unique child would need to be born either a man or woman; and, again, in a patriarchal culture, only a man could fulfill the role of Messiah, Lord, or Son of God. When one calls God personal, one can mean no more than that human personality is the best clue we have to the nature of God. Perhaps male personality is a better clue than female personality in a masculine-dominated society, but who would presume to project such sexual differentiation upon the very nature of God? The first of the Anglican Articles of Religion states that God is "without body, parts, or passions." To call God "he," implies no more than to call the entire human race "man" or "mankind."

The view that the female is a less true or complete image of God than the male is sometimes still supported by a tradition coming from Aristotle and St. Thomas Aquinas, which holds that woman is an incomplete human being, "a defective and/or misbegotten male." This tradition was based upon the prescientific biology which held that woman was an entirely passive partner in reproduction. On this subject, the Rev. Dr. Leonard Hodgson has commented, "We should be unwise to base our theological conclusions on notions of a prescientific biology which has never heard of genes or chromosomes."

Emotional and Psychological Pressures: The Commission is also aware that all the intellectual arguments against the ordination of women are connected with and reflect strong emotional and psychological pressures. These pressures *may* point to profound truth about men and women and their relationship to each other. Or, they *may* reflect magical notions of priesthood and Sacraments that linger on in the most sophisticated minds.

Or, they *may* reflect the fact that our deepest emotional experiences in the life of the Church, experiences often associated with the birth and baptism of children, maturity and Confirmation, worship and Sacraments, the pastoral ministry in times of crisis, joy and sorrow, are all closely associated with an episcopate and a priesthood that is exclusively male. Or, they *may* illustrate the sad fact that historical and psychological circumstances frequently make the Church the last refuge of the fearful and the timid in a changing world and that, the more rapidly the world changes, the stronger become the pressures to keep the Church safe and unchanged. Or, they *may* represent a threat to the present ordained ministers, to their wives, to lay men or lay women. The Commission is disturbed by the scorn, the indifference, the humorless levity, that is occasioned by the question of seating women in the House of Deputies, let alone their admission to ordination.

Finally, one cannot place much weight upon the common opinion that women themselves do not wish to be ordained. Who knows? Most women obviously do not, just as most men do not wish to become clergymen. But some women do. Kathleen Bliss has written, "This is not a woman's question, it is a Church question." The Church's answer must be determined, not primarily by what is good for woman, but what is good for the Church.

*   *   *

ANNEX C: THE 63RD GENERAL CONVENTION'S OPPORTUNITY TO COMPLETE THE OPENING OF THE PRIESTHOOD AND EPISCOPATE TO WOMEN AT HOUSTON, THROUGH INTERPRETATION (RATHER THAN AMENDMENT) OF THE CONSTITUTION, CANONS AND PRAYER BOOK ORDINAL

The 63rd General Convention can open the priesthood and episcopate to women without delay. In 1946 the House of Deputies opened its membership to a woman deputy. By passing one resolution to seat Mrs. Randolph H. Dyer of Missouri that House interpreted "Laymen" in Article I of the Constitution to be a generic word which included both males and females.

The 1970 Convention can interpret "Deacon," "Priest" and "Bishop" together with the referent pronouns "he," "his" and "him" to be generic words which include both males and females. Thus, by going the route of inclusive interpretation of words susceptible of such interpretation in the Constitution, Canons and Prayer Book Ordinal, this one Convention can affirm that women have equal rights with men to seek and accept ordering to the diaconate and priesthood and ordination and consecration to the episcopate; it can, further, affirm the right of the Church to ordain and consecrate women as well as men.

On the other hand, Convention can go the route taken by the House of Deputies in 1949. By opting to interpret the same word, "laymen," to be an exclusive word which did not include females, it refused to seat three women chosen as Deputies by their dioceses. By electing to go only the route of constitutional amendment to open its membership to women, that House forced the Church to wait 24 more years before its women members could be represented by one of their own sex.

The story of interpretation versus amendment of Constitution and Canons is succinctly told by excerpts from the Convention Journals of 1946 and 1949.

The Journal of General Convention, 1946 reports the action of the House of Deputies on page 102 as follows:

The Secretary inquired of the House if there were any objection to the seating of any member whose name was called. The Rev. Tom G. Akeley, of Maine, inquired what the rule might be in regard to seating in the House a woman who had been elected as a deputy. The Hon. Augustus N. Hand, of New York, said interpretation of "laymen," "person" and "man" in statutes was all inclusive. He moved that Mrs. Randolph H. Dyer of Missouri, be seated. Dr. Spencer Miller, Jr., of Newark, offered a substitute that the matter be referred to the Committee on Elections. Mr. A. D. Cochran of Oklahoma moved as a substitute for both motions that the seating of Mrs. Dyer be referred to the Committee on Constitution and Canons. The motion was lost. Mr. Anson T. McCook, of Connecticut, informed the House that if it wished a Canon dealing with such questions it could refer the matter to the Committee on

Canons, but meanwhile he called for Judge Hand's motion. Carried.

The action of the same House in 1949 is reported as follows on page 102 of the *Journal of General Convention, 1949*:

Resolved, That the women deputies from the following dioceses be not seated: Nebraska, Olympia, Missouri and Puerto Rico, as not eligible under Constitution, Article I, Section 4.
The resolution was adopted, 321 votes to 242.

If Convention wishes to open the priesthood and episcopate to women, it will also be faced with the choice of giving an inclusive or exclusive interpretation to "Deacon," "Priest," "Bishop," "man," "brother" and their referent pronouns in the Ordinal of the Prayer Book. Again, if it interprets them to exclude females, amendment of the language will be required.

There is a substantial difference, however, in revising the Prayer Book and amending the Constitution and Canons; Prayer Book revision is an even more formidable task. For example, almost from the time of its last revision in 1928 there has been a general consensus that the Office of Visitation of the Sick is unsatisfactory. The substantive changes that were needed would require the amendment of language which could only be made by revision of the Prayer Book. Revision is such a monumental undertaking, however, that the Office stands unchanged, just as it appeared in 1928.

On the other hand, changes in the Prayer Book can be easily made where the language is susceptible of fresh interpretation. This was illustrated by the action of the General Convention of 1949 relative to the use of intinction in the administration and reception of the Holy Communion. There has never been any question that administration of the wine from a common chalice, separate from the administration of the bread, is the only method of administration expressly intended and directed by the Prayer Book Offices and by Scripture and the unbroken tradition of the Church "from the Apostles' time."

Without altering any of the language of the Prayer Book Offices, however, the Convention of 1949 adopted a resolution permitting a bishop having jurisdiction to authorize intinction as an alternative method of administration (*Journal of General Convention, 1949*, pp. 263, 264).

SUMMARY: To summarize, the history of Convention's deliberations about intinction, like their deliberations about seating women in the House of Deputies, reflects a tacit agreement that the authors of neither the Prayer Book nor the Constitution contemplated such possibilities. Surely there is also agreement that the same authors did not contemplate the ordering of women to the priesthood nor their ordination and consecration to the episcopate.

There must also be agreement, however, that Convention has on many occasions treated the Prayer Book, the Constitution and the Canons as "living documents" which can be interpreted by simple resolutions to extend their provisions beyond the original intent, where the language was susceptible of such interpretation, without amending the language used.

Convention, then, will be faced with two possible questions:

1. Does the Convention *want* to open the priesthood and episcopate to women?

If the answer is "No," the matter is closed. If the answer is "Yes," a second question remains:

2. *What route* should be taken to open these orders to women?

The Joint Commission unanimously agrees that the only way to accomplish this purpose, in a fashion that is responsive to the need, is through adoption of the resolutions recommended at the outset of their Report.

In Canon 49, which was both amended and interpreted at Special Convention II to give women equal rights as licensed lay readers, an amendment was necessary to delete "male," a word which was obviously not susceptible of interpretation as a generic word which included both male and female. There are no such words used in the Ordinal, Constitution or Canons relative to ordination to the priesthood or consecration to the episcopate. The generic words which are used can all be interpreted and left unchanged at Houston, as the "he," "him" and "his" of Canon 49 were at South Bend.

*   *   *

AUTHORS'
NOTES

CHAPTER 1: *Looking Backward*

1. *Revised Interim Report of a Study on the Life and Work of Women in the Church* (Geneva: World Council of Churches, 1948), p. 18.

2. A poignant example of this hindrance is noted by Elsie Gibson in her book *When the Minister Is a Woman* (New York: Holt, Rinehart and Winston, 1970). She quotes an Episcopal laywoman, trained as a chaplain and working in a hospital: "When I call on patients . . . I am usually taken for a volunteer. . . . To try to explain my role is very awkward even if a patient is interested and asks. . . . How mystifying it would sound if I said that I was a certified church worker. . . . I would appreciate beyond measure the designation of 'chaplain.' My ministry would be made infinitely easier" (pp. 155–56).

3. C. S. Lewis, *God in the Dock: Essays on Theology and Ethics*, ed. Walter Hooper (Grand Rapids, Michigan: William B. Eerdmans, 1970), p. 239.

CHAPTER 2: *Woman's Place*

1. Dorothy L. Sayers, *Are Women Human?* (Downers Grove, Ill.: William B. Eerdmans, 1971), pp. 39–41.

2. Gunnar Myrdal, *An American Dilemma: The Negro Problem and Modern Democracy* (New York: Harper and Brothers, 1944), Appendix 5, p. 1077.

3. Cynthia F. Epstein, *Woman's Place: Options and Limits in Professional Careers* (Berkeley: University of California Press, 1971), p. 15.

4. Caroline Bird with Sara Welles Briller, *Born Female: The High Cost of Keeping Women Down*, rev. ed. (New York: David McKay, 1970), p. 44.

5. Epstein, p. 10.

6. Bird, p. 45.

7. Elizabeth Norris, *Feminine Figures, 1971* (New York: Communications Unit, National YWCA, n.d.).

8. Jonathan F. Stearns, "Discourse on Female Influence (1837)," *Up From the Pedestal: Selected Writings in the History of American Feminism*, ed. Aileen S. Kraditor (Chicago: Quadrangle Books, 1968), p. 49.

CHAPTER 3: *Anyplace but Here*

1. H. R. Hays, *The Dangerous Sex: The Myth of Feminine Evil* (New York: Pocket Books, 1972), p. 142.

CHAPTER 4: *The Manly Art of Self-Defense*

1. Sigmund Freud, quoted in Kate Millett, *Sexual Politics* (Garden City, N.Y.: Doubleday and Co., 1970), p. 178.

2. D. H. Lawrence, quoted in Sayers, *Are Women Human?* p. 33.

3. Karen Horney, *Feminine Psychology* (New York: W. W. Norton and Co., 1967), p. 136.

4. Erik H. Erikson, *Childhood and Society*, 2nd ed. (New York: W. W. Norton and Co., 1963), pp. 79–80.

5. Dr. Mead used this illustration in a talk given during a conference on women in the church, Synod House, Diocese of New York, April 24, 1971.

6. Hays, *The Dangerous Sex*, p. 271.

7. Biblical quotations here and throughout the book are from the Revised Standard Version.

8. This is the apparent implication in C. Kilmer Myer's assertion that "The Father begets the Son. This is essential to the *givingness* of the Christian Faith. . . ." Myers goes on to state that "Initiative is, in itself, a male rather than a female attribute." Though he does not say directly that he is speaking of initiative in the sex act, his emphasis on the Father's "begetting" of the Son leads one to conclude that Myers has sexual initiative in mind. See "Should Women Be Ordained? No," *The Episcopalian*, vol. 137, no. 2 (February, 1972), p. 8.

In fact, the (commonly-held) view that initiative in sexual relations is explicitly "male" ignores the wide range of sexual techniques and arrangements that people have employed in different times and places. In testimony to this range there is an extensive literature, from the *Kama Sutra* to anthropological studies to the more clinical observations of Kinsey and Masters and Johnson. Indeed, except in the case of rape, sexual initiative is never entirely male, for the female gives assent, at least. Folk wisdom knows well that sexual initiative is not wholly male, hence the time-worn joke about the bridegroom who says, "I chased her until she caught me."

9. The Gospel analogies to Christ as the bridegroom do not cast the disciples in the role of the bride, but rather in the role of wedding guests (e.g., Mark 2:19; Luke 5:34–35). In the Epistles, wedding imagery does cast the Church as bride (e.g., Ephesians 5:31–32).

Sally Cunneen quotes the Dutch theologian R. J. Bunnik, who reminds us that the bridegroom imagery is properly reserved for Christ and should not be extended to the priest: "The minister cannot be identified with the bridegroom of the Church. He belongs also to the female side of the comparison: as a member of the Church he is no less than any other Christian the bride."

See Sally Cunneen, *Sex: Female; Religion: Catholic* (New York: Holt, Rinehart and Winston, 1968), p. 142.

10. Hays, p. 271.

11. Margaretta K. Bowers, *Conflicts of the Clergy: A Psychodynamic Study with Case Histories* (New York: Thomas Nelson and Sons, 1964), p. 35.

CHAPTER 5: *Adam's Rib*

1. Richard Hooker, *The Ecclesiastical Polity*, Book V, Sec. 73.

2. Myers, "Should Women Be Ordained? No," p. 8.

3. E. L. Mascall, *Women and the Priesthood of the Church* (London: The Church Union, Church Literature Association, n.d.), p. 35.

4. Quoted in Cunneen, *Sex: Female; Religion: Catholic,* p. 139.

5. Krister Stendahl, *The Bible and the Role of Women: A Case Study in Hermeneutics,* trans. Emilie T. Sander (Philadelphia: Fortress Press, 1966), p. 38.

6. The discussion of the doctrine of subordination in I Corinthians 11 and 14 can be applied as well to the several other New Testament texts in which similar ideas are expressed; for example: Ephesians 5:22–24; Colossians 3:18; Titus 2:3–5.

7. Russell C. Prohl, *Woman in the Church: A Restudy of Woman's Place in Building the Kingdom* (Grand Rapids, Mich.: William B. Eerdmans, 1957), p. 38.

8. André Dumas, "Biblical Anthropology and the Participation of Women in the Ministry of the Church," *Concerning the Ordination of Women* (Geneva: World Council of Churches, 1964), p. 30.

9. See Prohl, pp. 51–54; Dumas, pp. 28–29; Derrick Sherwin Bailey, *Sexual Relation in Christian Thought* (New York: Harper and Brothers, 1959), p. 296.

10. Prohl, p. 37.

11. John Paul Boyer, "Some Thoughts on the Ordination of Women," *Ave: A Monthly Bulletin of the Church of St. Mary the Virgin, New York City,* Vol. XLI, No. 5 (May, 1972), p. 73.

12. *Ibid.*

13. Mascall, p. 13.

14. Stendahl, p. 40.

15. C. W. Atkinson, *A Position Paper in Favor of the Ordination of Women to the Priesthood in the Episcopal Church* (New York: n.d.), pp. 1–2; Stendahl, p. 32.

16. Atkinson, p. 2; Stendahl, pp. 35–37.

17. Krister Stendahl, "Women in the Churches: No Special Pleading," *Soundings,* Vol. LIII, No. 4 (Winter, 1970), p. 376.

18. Atkinson, p. 3.

19. Bailey, pp. 295–299.

CHAPTER 6: *Anatomy and Ministry*

1. Mascall, *Women and the Priesthood,* p. 34.

2. Stendahl, *The Bible and the Role of Women,* p. 38.

3. Albert J. duBois, "Why I am Against the Ordination of Women," *The Episcopalian,* Vol. 137, No. 7 (July, 1972), p. 22.

4. Myers, "Should Women Be Ordained? No," p. 8.

5. Boyer, "Some Thoughts on the Ordination of Women," p. 72.

6. The Book of Common Prayer, p. 603.

7. Alan Richardson, *Genesis 1–11: The Creation Stories and the Modern World View* (London: SCM Press, 1969), pp. 54–55.

8. Boyer, p. 72.

9. These and other instances of Jesus' "feminism" are discussed in Leonard Swidler, "Jesus the Liberator," *The Church Woman,* Vol. 38, No. 3 (March, 1972), pp. 14–16.

10. Boyer, pp. 74–75.

11. *Ibid.,* p. 75.

12. Leonard Hodgson, "Theological Objections to the Ordination of Women," *The Expository Times,* Vol. LXXVII, No. 7 (April, 1966), p. 211.

13. M. E. Thrall, *The Ordination of Women to the Priesthood: A Study of the Biblical Evidence* (London: SCM Press, 1958), pp. 87–89; Dumas, "Biblical Anthropology," p. 34.

14. Urban T. Holmes III, *The Future Shape of Ministry: A Theological Projection* (New York: The Seabury Press, 1971), p. 12.

15. *Ibid.,* p. 13.

16. F. C. Blomfield, quoted in Thrall, p. 102.

17. F. C. Blomfield, quoted in Mascall, p. 27.

18. Kenneth Escott Kirk, *Beauty and Bands and Other Papers* (Greenwich, Conn.: The Seabury Press, 1957), p. 182.

19. *Ibid.*

20. *Ibid.,* p. 186. For another view of the Christian marriage relation, see Bailey, *Sexual Relation in Christian Thought,* pp. 260–303.

21. Kirk, p. 181.

22. Swidler, p. 16.

23. The authorship of 1 Timothy is uncertain. See Paul Feine, Johannes Behm, Werner Georg Kümmel, *Introduction to the New Testament,* trans. A. J. Mattill, Jr., rev. ed. (New York: Abingdon, 1966), pp. 261–272.

24. Atkinson, *A Position Paper,* p. 2.

25. Dumas, p. 32.

26. *Ibid.,* p. 33.

27. *Ibid.,* pp. 32–33.

28. *Ibid.,* p. 33.

CHAPTER 7: *Times and Men's Manners*

1. *The Lambeth Conference, 1968: Resolutions and Reports* (London and New York: S.P.C.K. and The Seabury Press, 1968), p. 83.

2. *Ibid.,* p. 82.

3. *Ibid.*

4. Mascall, *Women and the Priesthood,* p. 35.

5. Williston Walker, *A History of the Christian Church* (rev. ed.; New York: Charles Scribner's Sons, 1959), p. 171.

6. Kenneth E. Kirk, *Conscience and Its Problems: An Introduction to Casuistry* (London: Longmans, Green and Co., 1927), p. 97. Jaroslav Pelikan notes, "Despite the thickness of various textbooks on dogma, the actual number of doctrines defined officially as binding *de jure* upon all believers is relatively small. . . . Even the doctrine of the death of Christ as vicarious satisfaction, while the common property of most Western theologians regardless of denomination, has never attained the dogmatic status of the doctrine of the two natures of Christ" [*Historical Theology: Continuity and Change in Christian Doctrine* (New York: Corpus, 1971), pp. 20–21].

7. Kirk, p. 97.

8. G. W. H. Lampe, "Church Tradition and the Ordination of Women," *The Expository Times,* Vol. LXXVI, No. 4 (January, 1965), p. 123.

9. *Ibid.,* p. 124.

10. *Ibid.*

11. For an argument against women in Holy Orders based on such a canon, see George B. Armstrong, "The Impossibility of Ordaining Women," *The American Church News*, Vol. XXXVII, No. 1 (Lent, 1972), p. 9.

12. *E.g.*: Tertullian, "Do you not know that you are Eve? . . . You are the Devil's gateway. . . . How easily you destroyed man, the image of God. Because of the death which you brought upon us, even the Son of God had to die," quoted in Mary Daly, *The Church and the Second Sex* (New York: Harper and Row, 1968), p. 45; Epiphanius, ". . . a feeble race, untrustworthy and of mediocre intelligence," quoted in Lampe, p. 124.

13. J. Robert Wright, "Yes, Ordain Women," *The Episcopal New Yorker*, Vol. XLVIII, No. 6 (June, 1972), p. 2.

14. Hodgson, "Theological Objections to the Ordination of Women," p. 213.

15. *Ibid.*

16. Kirk, p. 92.

17. The Book of Common Prayer, p. 609.

18. *The Lambeth Conference, 1968*, p. 106.

CHAPTER 8: *The Practices of the Churches of God*

1. R. W. Howard, *Should Women Be Priests? Three Sermons Preached before the University of Oxford* (Oxford: Basil Blackwell, 1949), p. 42.

2. This information is compiled from the *Yearbook of American Churches: Information on All Faiths in the U.S.A.* (New York: Council Press, 1971), pp. 177–188 and from *Women in the Church* (A Statement by the Worship and Mission Section of the Roman Catholic/Presbyterian—Reformed Consultation, Richmond, Virginia, October 30, 1971), Appendix, passim. The latter document is an accurate and up-to-date account of the status of women in nine American churches and in the proposals for the Church of Christ Uniting (COCU) and may be obtained for $2.00 per copy from the Rev. Raymond V. Kearns, 475 Riverside Drive, Room 918, New York, NY 10027.

3. It is interesting to note that even in denominations where ordination is open to women, there has not been a great rush of women into the clergy. Of the 91 women who graduated from United Presbyterian seminaries between 1960 and 1970, only 32 have been ordained (*Report of the Task Force on Women to the 183rd General Assembly, 1971*). Less than 3 percent of United Church of Christ ministers are women. The two Lutheran synods that voted in 1970 to ordain women have ordained only three women at this writing. These statistics are explained in part by the fact that some churches, especially Lutheran churches, will not ordain a person who does not have a church-related job, or "call." Qualified women have found difficulty in locating parishes that will call them.

4. Lukas Vischer, "The Ordination of Women," *Concerning the Ordination of Women*, p. 4.

5. *What Is Ordination Coming To?* (Report of a Consultation on the Ordination of Women held in Cartigny, Geneva, Switzerland, 21st–26th September 1970), ed. Brigalia Bam (Geneva: World Council of Churches, 1970), p. 59.

6. *Ibid.*, p. 72.

7. *Ibid.*, p. 51.

8. *Ibid.*, p. 1.

9. Myers, "Should Women Be Ordained? No," pp. 8–9.

10. Daly, *The Church and the Second Sex*, p. 87.

11. *Ibid.*, pp. 103–104.

12. "Woman's Right to Full Participation Upheld by Bishops' Synod," *Genesis III: Philadelphia Task Force on Women in Religion*, vol. I, no. 5 (January–February, 1972), p. 1.

13. "Women: 'Equality Depends on Study,'" *The National Catholic Reporter*, vol. 8, no. 25 (April 21, 1972), p. 17.

14. Wright, "Yes, Ordain Women," p. 3.

15. *Women in the Church*, pp. vii–x.

16. *Ibid.*, pp. ix–x.

17. Nicolae Chitescu, "The Ordination of Women: A Comment on the Attitude of the Orthodox Church," *Concerning the Ordination of Women*, p. 57.

18. *Ibid.*, passim.

19. Wright, p. 2.

CHAPTER 9: *"Yes, But . . ."*

1. *The Church Annual* (New York: Morehouse Barlow, 1960), Summary of Statistics, p. 6; *The Church Annual* (New York: Morehouse Barlow, 1972), Summary of Statistics, p. 8.

2. "Progress Report to the House of Bishops from The Committee to Study the Proper Place of Women in the Ministry of the Church, October, 1966," *Journal of the General Convention of the Protestant Episcopal Church in the United States of America, 1967*, Appendix 35.8.

3. Stephen F. Bayne, unpublished paper "Reflections on the Ministry," p. 1.

4. "UTO for Lobby Funds," *American Church News*, vol. XXXVII, no. 2 (Ascension, 1972), p. 4.

5. Margaret Sittler Ermarth notes clergy resistance to the ordination of women in a number of denominations in *Adam's Fractured Rib: Observations on Women in the Church* (Philadelphia: Fortress Press, 1970), passim. Elsie Gibson also observes that in the Episcopal Church especially the clergy are anxious to blame the laity for our failure to ordain women priests (*When the Minister Is a Woman*, p. 30). Sally Cunneen found in a survey among Roman Catholics that more priests than lay people opposed ordination for women (*Sex: Female; Religion: Catholic*, pp. 130–146).

6. For a brief discussion of this phenomenon, see Gibson, pp. 26–30. Four of the ordained women who responded to Gibson's survey were formerly Episcopalians, who left the Episcopal Church to be ordained elsewhere. One was one of the first woman graduates of Virginia Theological Seminary.

EPILOGUE: *Do Not Quench the Spirit*

1. The Rt. Rev. John A. T. Robinson, quoted in Cecil Northcott, "Woolwich's Revolution," *The Christian Century*, vol. LXXXI, no. 21 (May 20, 1964), p. 678.

FOR FURTHER READING

THE DEBATE WITHIN ANGLICANISM
ON WOMEN IN HOLY ORDERS

For the Ordination of Women:

HODGSON, L. "Theological Objections to the Ordination of Women," *The Expository Times,* LXXVII, 7 (April, 1966), pp. 210–213.

LAMPE, G. W. H. "Church Tradition and the Ordination of Women," *The Expository Times,* LXXVI, 4 (January, 1965), pp. 123–125.

THRALL, M. E. *The Ordination of Women to the Priesthood: A Study of the Biblical Evidence.* London: SCM Press, 1958.

TROTT, FRANCES. "The Priesthood Is for Man (Both Sexes of Him)," *The Episcopalian,* 137, 8 (August, 1972), pp. 11, 26–27.

WOLF, WILLIAM J. "Should Women Be Ordained? Yes," *The Episcopalian,* 137, 2 (February, 1972), pp. 9–11.

WRIGHT, J. ROBERT. "Yes, Ordain Women," *The Episcopal New Yorker,* XLVIII, 6 (June, 1972), pp. 2–3.

Against the Ordination of Women:

DUBOIS, ALBERT J. "Why I am Against the Ordination of Women," *The Episcopalian,* 137, 7 (July, 1972), pp. 21–23, 30.

KIRK, KENNETH ESCOTT. "The Ordination of Women," *Beauty and Bands and Other Papers.* Greenwich, Conn.: The Seabury Press, 1957, pp. 177–188.

LEWIS, C. S. "Priestesses in the Church?" *God in the Dock: Es-*

says on *Theology and Ethics*, ed. Walter Hooper. Grand Rapids, Mich.: William B. Eerdmans, 1970, pp. 234–239.

MASCALL, E. L. *Women and the Priesthood of the Church.* London: The Church Union, Church Literature Association, n.d.

MYERS, C. KILMER. "Should Women Be Ordained? No," *The Episcopalian*, 137, 2 (February, 1972), pp. 8–9.

WILLIAMS, N. P. "Deaconesses and Holy Orders," *N. P. Williams*, ed. Eric Waldram Kemp. London: S.P.C.K., 1954, pp. 185–201.

OFFICIAL STUDIES AND REPORTS
ON WOMEN AND MINISTRY

Concerning the Ordination of Women. Geneva: World Council of Churches, 1964.

The Ordination of Women. A Report Distributed by Authorization of the Church Body Presidents as a Contribution to Further Study, Based on Materials Produced Through the Division of Theological Studies of the Lutheran Council, U.S.A. Condensed by Raymond Tiemeyer, n.p. Augsburg, 1970.

"Progress Report to the House of Bishops from The Committee to Study the Proper Place of Women in the Ministry of the Church, October, 1966," *Journal of the General Convention of the Protestant Episcopal Church in the United States of America*, 1967, Appendix 35.4–35.12.

"Report of the Joint Commission on Ordained and Licensed Ministries," *Journal of the General Convention of the Protestant Episcopal Church in the United States of America*, 1970, pp. 532–539.

What Is Ordination Coming To? Report of a Consultation on the Ordination of Women held in Cartigny, Geneva, Switzerland, 21st–26th September, 1970. Edited by Brigalia Bam. Geneva: World Council of Churches, 1971.

Women and Holy Orders. Being the Report of a Commission appointed by the Archbishops of Canterbury and York. London: Church Information Office, 1966.

"Women and the Priesthood," *The Lambeth Conference, 1968: Resolutions and Reports.* London and New York: S.P.C.K. and The Seabury Press, 1968, pp. 106–108.

Women in the Church. A Statement by the Worship and Mission Section of the Roman Catholic/Presbyterian–Reformed Consultation. Richmond, Virginia, October 30, 1971.

WOMEN IN THE CHURCH: OTHER STUDIES

BLISS, KATHLEEN. *The Service and Status of Women in the Churches.* London: SCM Press, 1952.

CULVER, ELSIE THOMAS. *Women in the World of Religion.* Garden City, New York: Doubleday, 1967.

CUNNEEN, SALLY. *Sex: Female; Religion: Catholic.* New York: Holt, Rinehart and Winston, 1968.

DALY, MARY. *The Church and the Second Sex.* New York: Harper and Row, 1968.

DOELY, SARAH BENTLEY (ed.). *Women's Liberation and the Church.* New York: Association Press, 1970.

ERMARTH, MARGARET SITTLER. *Adam's Fractured Rib: Observations on Women in the Church.* Philadelphia: Fortress Press, 1970.

STENDAHL, KRISTER. *The Bible and the Role of Women: A Case Study in Hermeneutics.* Emilie T. Sander (trans.). Philadelphia: Fortress Press, 1966.